Yc

COACHING YOUTH

CRICKET

Australian Cricket Board

Library of Congress Cataloging-in-Publication Data

Australian Cricket Board.
  Coaching youth cricket / Australian Cricket Board.
    p.   cm.
  ISBN 0-7360-3330-0
    1. Cricket for children--Coaching--Australia.   I. Title.
  GV929.3 .A78   2000
  796.358'07'7--dc21   00-040879

ISBN: 0-7360-3330-0

Acquisitions Editor: Tom Hanlon; **Managing Editor**: Leigh LaHood; **Copyeditor**: Barbara Walsh; **Proofreader**: Lois Lasater; **Graphic Designers**: Judy Henderson and Stuart Cartwright; **Graphic Artist**: Sandra Meier; **Cover Designer**: Stuart Cartwright; **Photographer (cover)**: © Action Images; **Illustrators**: illustrations on pages v, 3, 4, 6, 9, 11, 26, 27, 31, and 44 by Tim Stiles; figures 5.10 and 5.11 by Sharon Smith; all other illustrations by Robert Wood; **Printer**: United Graphics

Copies of this book are available at special discounts for bulk purchase for sales promotions, premiums, fund-raising, or educational use. Special editions or book excerpts can also be created to specifications. For details, contact the Special Sales Manager at Human Kinetics.

Printed in the United States of America   10   9   8   7   6   5   4

Human Kinetics
Web site: www.HumanKinetics.com

United States: Human Kinetics
P.O. Box 5076
Champaign, IL 61825-5076
800-747-4457
e-mail: humank@hkusa.com

Canada: Human Kinetics
475 Devonshire Road, Unit 100
Windsor, ON N8Y 2L5
800-465-7301 (in Canada only)
e-mail: orders@hkcanada.com

Europe: Human Kinetics
107 Bradford Road
Stanningley
Leeds LS28 6AT, United Kingdom
+44 (0)113 255 5665
e-mail: hk@hkeurope.com

Australia: Human Kinetics
57A Price Avenue
Lower Mitcham, South Australia 5062
08 8277 1555
e-mail: liaw@hkaustralia.com

New Zealand: Human Kinetics
Division of Sports Distributors NZ Ltd.
P.O. Box 300 226 Albany
North Shore City, Auckland
0064 9 448 1207
e-mail: blairc@hknewz.com

Contents

A Message From the Australian Cricket Board

Welcome to Coaching!

A Message From the Australian Cricket Board

The Australian Cricket Board (ACB) is the national governing body for cricket in Australia. In cooperation with the state associations, the ACB is responsible for coaching, development, and administration of the game throughout the nation.

Coaching Youth Cricket is a useful resource for beginning coaches as well as experienced coaches looking to enhance their coaching skills. The practical, sequential information provided will prepare coaches for communicating basic cricketing skills to young people.

This book covers areas such as the role of coaches, effective communication, and how to introduce new skills. Other topics include training methods, how to identify and correct faults in technique, how to promote leadership and team spirit, sport science concepts, and basic first aid.

By following the information provided in this book, coaches will be able to instill in young players the ideals of teamwork, fitness, and friendship as part of a fun learning environment. A coach can be the most important person in a young player's life; the ACB embraces publications such as *Coaching Youth Cricket* as a means of communicating the basics of the game to those who have a great impact on the lives of young athletes.

Welcome to coaching, and be ready to discover the personal satisfaction that comes from working closely with our nation's future—its children.

Welcome to Coaching!

Coaching young people is an exciting way to be involved in sport. But it isn't easy. Some coaches are overwhelmed by the responsibilities involved in helping young players through their early sport experiences. And that's not surprising, because coaching youngsters requires more than bringing the cricket gear, putting up the stumps, and letting them play. It involves preparing them mentally and physically to compete effectively, fairly, and safely in their sport, and providing them with a positive role model.

This book will help you meet the challenges *and* experience the many rewards of coaching young players. We call it *Coaching Youth Cricket* because it is intended for adults who have little or no formal participation in coaching cricket. In this book you'll learn how to apply general coaching principles and teach cricket rules, skills, and strategies successfully to children. And while you may find that some of the information does not apply to your junior cricket programme, we're confident this book will help you get a good jump on your coaching career.

The American Sport Education Program (ASEP) thanks the Australian Cricket Board and the State and Territory Cricket Associations for contributing their cricket expertise to this book. Combined with ASEP's material on important coaching principles, this book covers all bases.

This book also serves as a text for the Level 1 coaches' courses. If you would like more information about this course, contact your State or Territory Cricket Association.

ASEP
P.O. Box 5076
Champaign, IL 61825-5076
1-800-747-5698

Good coaching!

Unit 1

Who, Me . . . a Coach?

If you are like most new coaches, you have probably been recruited from the ranks of concerned parents, sport enthusiasts, or community volunteers. And, like many novice and veteran coaches, you probably had little formal instruction on how to coach. But when the call went out for coaches to assist with the local youth cricket programme, you answered because you like children and enjoy cricket, and perhaps are interested in starting a coaching career.

I Want to Help, But . . .

Your initial coaching assignment may be difficult. Like many volunteers, you may not know everything there is to know about cricket, nor about how to work with children between the ages of 8 and 16. Relax, because *Coaching Youth Cricket* will help you learn the basics for coaching cricket effectively. In the coming pages you will find the answers to such common questions as these:

- What tools do I need to be a good coach?
- How can I best communicate with my players?
- How do I go about teaching sport skills?
- What can I do to promote safety?
- What should I do when someone is injured?
- What are the basic rules, skills, and strategies of cricket?
- What practice drills will improve my players' cricket skills?

Before answering these questions, let's take a look at what's involved in being a coach.

Am I a Parent or a Coach?

Many coaches are parents, but the two roles should not be confused. Unlike your role as a parent, as a coach you are responsible not only to yourself and your child, but also to the organisation, all the players on the team (including your child), and their parents. Because of this additional responsibility, your behaviour on the cricket field will be different from your behaviour at home, and your son or daughter may not understand why.

For example, imagine the confusion of a young boy who is the center of his parents' attention at home but is barely noticed by his father/coach in the sport setting. Or consider the mixed signals received by a young girl whose cricket skill is constantly evaluated by a mother/coach who otherwise rarely comments on her daughter's activities. You need to explain to your son or daughter your new responsibilities and how they will affect your relationship when coaching.

Take the following steps to avoid such problems in coaching your child:

- Ask your child if he or she wants you to coach the team.
- Explain why you wish to be involved with the team.
- Discuss with your child how your interactions will change when you take on the role of coach at practice or games.
- Limit your coaching behaviour to when you are in the coaching role.
- Avoid parenting during practice or game situations to keep your role clear in your child's mind.
- Reaffirm your love for your child, irrespective of his or her performance on the cricket field.

What Are My Responsibilities as a Coach?

A coach assumes the responsibility of doing everything possible to ensure that the youngsters on his or her team will have an enjoyable and safe sporting experience while they learn sport skills. If you're ever in doubt about your approach, remind yourself that 'fun and fundamentals' are most important.

Provide an Enjoyable Experience

Cricket should be fun. Even if nothing else is accomplished, make certain your players have fun. Take the fun out of sport and you'll take the kids out of sport.

Children enter sport for a number of reasons (e.g., to meet and play with other children, to develop physically, and to learn skills), but their major objective is to have fun. Help them satisfy this goal by injecting humour and variety into your practices. Also, make games nonthreatening, festive experiences for your players. Such an approach will increase your players' desire to participate in the future, which should be the biggest goal of youth sport. Unit 2 will help you learn how to satisfy your players' yearning for fun and keep winning in perspective. And unit 3 will describe how you can effectively communicate this perspective to them.

Provide a Safe Experience

You are responsible for planning and teaching activities in such a way that the progression between activities minimises risks (see units 4 and 5). Further, you must ensure that the field on which your team practises and plays and the equipment team members use are free of hazards. Finally, you need to protect yourself from any legal liability issues that might arise from your involvement as a coach. Unit 5 will help you take the appropriate precautions.

Provide Opportunities for Children With Disabilities

There's a possibility that a child with a disability of some kind will register for your team. Don't panic! A number of organisations can provide you with information to help you best meet this child's needs.

As a coach, you need to know about the laws that give individuals the same legal protection against discrimination on the basis of disabilities as is provided against discrimination on the basis of race, gender, and class. The law does recognise that there are times when including an individual who is disabled might risk the safety of that individual and other players, but the exact way that courts are treating such antidiscrimination acts is still being decided. In general, the law requires that reasonable accommodations be made to include children with disabilities into organised sport programs. If a parent or child approaches you on the subject, and you aren't sure what to do, talk to the junior coordinator in charge of your cricket programme. If you make a decision on your own pertaining to discrimination, you may be vulnerable to a lawsuit. Your local government may be able to direct you as to the process you should follow.

Keep in mind that these children want to participate alongside their able-bodied peers. Give them the same support and encouragement that you give other players, and model their inclusion and acceptance for all your players.

Teach Basic Cricket Skills

In becoming a coach, you take on the role of educator. You must teach your players the fundamental skills and strategies necessary for success in cricket. That means that you meed to 'go to school'.

If you don't know the basics of cricket now, you can learn them by reading the second half of this book, units 6, 7, and 8. But even if you know cricket as a player, do you know how to teach it? This book will help you get started. There are also many valuable cricket books on the market.

You'll also find it easier to provide good educational experiences for your players if you plan your practices. Refer to Unit 4 for assistance in this area.

Getting Help

Experienced coaches in your association are an especially good source of help for you. These coaches have all experienced the same emotions and concerns you are facing, and their advice and feedback can be invaluable as you work through your first season. Regional Development Officers and Cricket Managers from your state governing body are also a resource that can provide you with assistance.

You can also learn a lot by watching matches on television. You might even ask a few of the coaches you respect most to lend you a hand with a couple of your practices. You can get additional help by attending cricket clinics, reading cricket publications, and studying instructional videos. In addition to the Australian Cricket Board (ACB), the following State and Territory organisations will assist you in obtaining more cricket coaching information:

Cricket New South Wales
Brian Hughes, CEO
Sydney Cricket Ground
Driver Avenue
P.O. Box 333
Paddington
NSW 2021
Tel 02 9339 0999
Fax 02 9331 1555
e-mail: nswca@cricket.org
Internet: **www.cricket-nsw.
cricket.org**

Queensland Cricket Association
Graham Dixon, CEO
1 Bogan Street
Breakfast Creek
P.O. Box 575
Albion
QLD 4010
Tel 07 3293 3100
Fax 07 3262 9160
e-mail: qldc@qld.cricket.com.au
Internet: **www.qldcricket.com.au**

**South Australian Cricket
Association**
Mike Deare, CEO
Adelaide Oval
North Adelaide
SA 5006
Tel 08 8300 3800
Fax 08 8231 4346
e-mail: admin@saca.com.au
Internet: **www.saca.com.au**

Tasmanian Cricket Association
David Johnston, CEO
Bellerive Oval
Derwent Street
Bellerive
P.O. Box 495
Rosny Park
TAS 7018
Tel 03 6244 7099
Fax 03 6244 3924

Victorian Cricket Association
Ken Jacobs, CEO
86 Jolimont Street
Jolimont
P.O. Box 327
East Melbourne
VIC 3002
Tel 03 9653 1100
Fax 03 9653 1196
e-mail: vca@viccricket.asn.au
Internet: **www.viccricket.asn.au**

**Western Australian Cricket
Association**
Mike Allenby, CEO
WACA Ground
Nelson Crescent
East Perth
WA 6004
P.O. Box 6045
East Perth
WA 6892
Tel 08 9265 7222
Fax 08 9221 1823
Internet:
www.westernwarriors.com.au

**Northern Territory Cricket
 Association**
Jim Ford, CEO
Marrara Cricket Ground
Abala Road
Marrara
NT 0812
P.O. Box 40895
Casuarina
NT 0801
Tel 08 8927 0444
Fax 08 8927 0306
e-mail: ntca@topend.com.au

**Australian Capital Territory
 Cricket Assocation**
Gary Goodman, CEO
Cricket Cottage
Manuka Oval
P.O. Box 3379
Manuka
ACT 2603
Tel 02 6239 6002
Fax 02 6295 7135
e-mail: actcricket@interact.net.au

Womens Cricket Australia
Sue Crow, Executive Director
c/o Australian Cricket Board
e-mail: wcaust@bigpond.com
Internet: **wwwausport.gov.au/
 wca**

Coaching cricket is a rewarding experience. And, just as you want your players to learn and practise to be the best they can be, you need to learn all you can about coaching in order to be the best cricket coach you can be.

What Tools Do I Need as a Coach?

Have you purchased the traditional coaching tools—things like whistles, bats, balls, appropriate footwear, and a clipboard? They'll help you coach, but to be a successful coach, you'll need five other tools that cannot be bought. These tools are available only through self-examination and hard work; they're easy to remember using the acronym COACH:

C—Comprehension
O—Outlook
A—Affection
C—Character
H—Humour

Comprehension

Comprehension of the rules, skills, and tactics of cricket is required. To help you learn about the game, the second half of this book describes how cricket is played as well as specific techniques and strategies. In the cricket-specific section of this book, you'll also find a variety of drills to use in developing young players' skills. And, perhaps most important, you'll learn how to apply your knowledge of the game to teach your cricket team.

To improve your comprehension of cricket, take the following steps:

- Read the cricket-specific section of this book.
- Read other cricket coaching books.
- Contact any of the organisations on pages 7–8.
- Attend cricket coaches' clinics and gain coaching accreditation.
- Talk with other, more experienced, cricket coaches.
- Observe local senior and junior games.
- Watch televised cricket matches.

In addition to having cricket knowledge, you must implement proper training and safety methods so your players can participate with little risk of injury. Even then, sport injuries will occur. And more often than not, you'll be the first person responding to your players' injuries, so be sure you understand the basic emergency care procedures described in unit 5. Also, read in that unit how to handle more serious sport injury situations.

Outlook

Outlook refers to your perspective and goals—what you are seeking as a coach. The most common coaching objectives are (a) to have

fun, (b) to help players develop their physical, mental, and social skills, and (c) to win. Thus your outlook involves the priorities you set, your planning, and your vision for the future.

To work successfully with children in a sport setting, you must have your priorities in order. In just what order do you rank the importance of fun, development, and winning?

Answer the following questions to examine your objectives:

Which situation would you be most proud of?
   a. Knowing that each participant enjoyed playing cricket.
   b. Seeing that all players improved their cricket skills.
   c. Winning the local championship.

Which statement best reflects your thoughts about sport?
   a. If it isn't fun, don't do it.
   b. Everyone should learn something every day.
   c. Sport isn't fun if you don't win.

How would you like your players to remember you?
   a. As a coach who was fun to play for.
   b. As a coach who provided a good base of fundamental skills.
   c. As a coach who had a winning record.

Which would you most like to hear a parent of a child on your team say?
   a. Billy really had a good time playing cricket this year.
   b. Susie learned some important lessons playing cricket this year.
   c. Jack played for the premier cricket team this year.

Which of the following would be the most rewarding moment of your season?
   a. Having your team want to continue playing, even after practice is over.
   b. Seeing one of your players finally master a skill that had previously eluded him or her.
   c. Winning the local competition.

Look over your answers. If you most often selected 'a' responses, then having fun is most important to you. A majority of 'b' answers suggests that skill development is what attracts you to coaching. And if 'c' was your most frequent response, winning is tops on your list of coaching priorities.

Most coaches say fun and development are more important, but when it actually comes to coaching, some coaches emphasise—indeed, overemphasise—winning. You, too, will face situations that challenge you to keep winning in its proper perspective. During such moments, you'll have to choose between emphasising your players' development or winning. If your priorities are in order, your players' well-being will take precedence over your team's win-loss record every time.

Take the following actions to better define your outlook:

1. Determine your priorities for the season.
2. Prepare for situations that challenge your priorities.
3. Set goals for yourself and your players that are consistent with those priorities.
4. Plan how you and your players can best attain those goals.
5. Review your goals frequently to be sure that you are staying on track.

It is particularly important for coaches to permit all young players to participate. Each youngster—male or female, small or tall, gifted or disabled—should have an opportunity to develop skills and have fun.

Remember that the challenge and joy of sport is experienced through striving to win, not through winning itself. Players who rarely get to bat or bowl or who are regularly made the reserve are denied the opportunity to strive to win. And herein lies the irony: coaches who allow all of their players to participate and develop skills will—in the end—come out on top.

ASEP has a motto that will help you keep your outlook in the best interest of the kids on your team. It summarises in four words all you need to remember when establishing your coaching priorities:

Athletes First,

Winning Second.

This motto recognises that striving to win is an important, even vital, part of sport. But it emphatically states that no efforts in striving to win should be made at the expense of the players' well-being, development, and enjoyment.

Affection

Affection is another vital tool you will want to have in your coaching kit: a genuine concern for the young people you coach. It involves having a love for children, a desire to share with them your love and knowledge of cricket, and the patience and understanding that allow each athlete playing for you to grow from his or her involvement in cricket.

Successful coaches have a real concern for the health and welfare of their players. They care that each child on the team has an enjoyable and successful experience. They recognise that there are similarities between young people's sport experiences and other activities in their lives, and they encourage their players to strive to learn from all their experiences to become well-rounded individuals. These coaches have a strong desire to work with children and be involved in their growth. And they have the patience to work with those who are slower to learn or less capable of performing. If you have such qualities or are willing to work hard to develop them, then you have the affection necessary to coach young athletes.

There are many ways to demonstrate your affection and patience, including these:

- Make an effort to get to know each player on your team.
- Treat each player as an individual.
- Empathise with players trying to learn new and difficult cricket skills.
- Treat players as you would like to be treated under similar circumstances.
- Be in control of your emotions.
- Show your enthusiasm for being involved with your team.
- Keep a cheerful and positive tone in all of your communications.

Some children appreciate a pat on the back or shoulder as a sign of your approval or affection. But be aware that not all players feel comfortable with being touched. When this is the case, you need to respect their wishes.

Character

Character is a word that adults use frequently in conversations about sport experiences and young people. If you haven't already, you may one day be asked to explain whether you think sport builds good character. What will you say?

The fact that you have decided to coach young cricketers probably means that you think participation in sport is important. But whether or not that participation develops character in your players depends as much on you as it does on the sport itself. How can you build character in your players?

Youngsters learn by listening to what adults say. But they learn even more by watching the behaviour of certain important individuals. As a coach, you are likely to be a significant figure in the lives of your players. Will you be a good role model?

Having good character means modeling appropriate behaviours for sport and life. That means more than just saying the right things. What you say and what you do must match. There is no place in coaching for the 'Do as I say, not as I do' philosophy. Challenge, support, encourage, and reward every child, and your players will

be more likely to accept, even celebrate, their differences. Be in control before, during, and after all games and practices. And don't be afraid to admit that you were wrong. No one is perfect!

Many of us have been coached by someone who believes that criticising players is a good way to build character. In reality, this approach damages children's self-esteem and teaches them that their value as a person is based on how they perform in sport. Unit 3 will help you communicate with your players in a way that builds positive self-esteem and develops your players' skills.

Finally, take stock of your own attitudes about ethnic, gender, and other stereotypes. You are an individual coach, and it would be wrong for others to form beliefs about you based on their personal attitudes about coaches in general. Similarly, you need to avoid making comments that support stereotypes of others. Let your words and actions show your players that every individual matters, and you will be teaching them a valuable lesson about respecting and supporting individual differences.

Consider the following steps to being a good role model:

- Take stock of your strengths and weaknesses.
- Build on your strengths.
- Set goals for yourself to improve those areas you would not like to see mimicked.
- If you slip up, apologise to your team and to yourself. You'll do better next time.

Humour

Humour is an often-overlooked coaching tool. For our use it means having the ability to laugh at yourself and with your players during practices and games. Nothing helps balance the tone of a serious, skill-learning session like a chuckle or two. And a sense of humour puts in perspective the many mistakes your young players will make. So don't get upset over each miscue or respond negatively to erring players. Allow your players and yourself to enjoy the ups, and don't dwell on the downs.

Here are some tips for injecting humour into your practices:

- Make practices fun by including a variety of activities.
- Keep all players involved in drills and minor games.
- Consider laughter by your players a sign of enjoyment, not waning discipline.
- Smile!

Where Do You Stand?

To take stock of your 'coaching tool kit', rank yourself on the three questions for each of the five coaching tools. Simply circle the number that best describes your current status on each item.

Not at all		Somewhat		Very much so
1	**2**	**3**	**4**	**5**

Comprehension _____

1.	Could you explain the rules of cricket to other parents without studying for a long time?	1 2 3 4 5
2.	Do you know how to organise and conduct safe cricket practices?	1 2 3 4 5
3.	Do you know how to provide first aid for most common, minor sport injuries?	1 2 3 4 5

Comprehension Score: _____

Outlook

4. Do you place the interests of all children ahead of winning when you coach?   1 2 3 4 5

5. Do you plan for every meeting, practice, and game?   1 2 3 4 5

6. Do you have a vision of what you want your players to be able to do by the end of the season?   1 2 3 4 5

Outlook Score: _____

Affection

7. Do you enjoy working with children?   1 2 3 4 5

8. Are you patient with youngsters learning new skills?   1 2 3 4 5

9. Are you able to show your players that you care?   1 2 3 4 5

Affection Score: _____

Character

10. Are your words and behaviours consistent with each other?   1 2 3 4 5

11. Are you a good model for your players?   1 2 3 4 5

12. Do you keep negative emotions under control before, during, and after games?   1 2 3 4 5

Character Score: _____

Humour

13. Do you usually smile at your players?   1 2 3 4 5

14. Are your practices fun?   1 2 3 4 5

15. Are you able to laugh at your mistakes?   1 2 3 4 5

Humour Score: _____

If you scored 9 or less on any of the coaching tools, be sure to reread those sections carefully. And even if you score 15 on each tool, don't be complacent. Keep learning! Then you'll be well equipped with the tools you need to coach young cricketers.

Unit 3

How Should I Communicate With My Players?

Now you know the tools needed to COACH: Comprehension, Outlook, Affection, Character, and Humour. These are the essentials for effective coaching; without them, you'd have a difficult time getting started. But none of those tools will work if you don't know how to use them with your players—and this requires skilful communication. This unit examines what communication is and how you can become a more effective communicator-coach.

What's Involved in Communication?

Coaches often mistakenly believe that communication involves only instructing players to do something, but verbal commands are a very small part of the communication process. More than half of what is communicated is nonverbal. So remember when you are coaching: actions often speak louder than words.

Communication in its simplest form involves two people: a sender and a receiver. The sender transmits the message verbally, through facial expression, and possibly through body language. Once the message is sent, the receiver must try to determine the meaning of the message. A receiver who fails to attend or listen will miss parts, if not all, of the message.

How Can I Send More Effective Messages?

Young cricketers often have little understanding of the rules and skills of cricket and probably even less confidence in playing it. So they need accurate, understandable, and supportive messages to help them along. That's why your verbal and nonverbal messages are so important.

Verbal Messages

'Sticks and stones may break my bones, but words will never hurt me' isn't true. Spoken words can have a strong and long-lasting effect.

And coaches' words are particularly influential because youngsters place great importance on what coaches say. Perhaps you, like many former youth sport participants, have a difficult time remembering much of anything you were told by your elementary school teachers but can still recall several specific things your coaches at that level said to you. Such is the lasting effect of a coach's comments to a player.

Whether you are correcting misbehaviour, teaching a player how to field ground balls, or praising a player for good effort, there are a number of things you should consider when sending a message verbally. They include the following:

- Be positive and honest.
- State it clearly and simply.
- Say it loud enough, and say it again.
- Be consistent.

Be Positive and Honest

Nothing turns people off like hearing someone nag all the time, and young players react similarly to a coach who gripes constantly. Kids particularly need encouragement because many of them doubt their ability to play cricket. So look for and tell your players what they did well.

But don't cover up poor or incorrect play with rosy words of praise. Kids know all too well when they've erred, and no cheerfully expressed cliché can undo their mistakes. If you fail to acknowledge players' errors, they will think you are insincere.

State It Clearly and Simply

Positive and honest messages are good, but only if expressed directly in words your players understand. 'Beating around the bush' is ineffective and inefficient. And if you do ramble, your players will miss the point of your message and probably lose interest. Here are some tips for saying things clearly:

- Organise your thoughts before speaking to your players.
- Explain things thoroughly, but don't bore them with long-winded monologues.

- Use language your players can understand. However, avoid trying to use their age group's slang vocabulary.

COMPLIMENT SANDWICH

A good way to handle situations in which you have identified and must correct improper technique is to serve your players a 'compliment sandwich':

1. Point out what the player did correctly.

2. Let the player know what was incorrect in the performance and instruct him or her how to correct it.

3. Encourage the player by reemphasising what he or she did well.

Say It Loud Enough, and Say It Again

A cricket ground with kids spread out from deep fine leg to mid on can make communication difficult. So talk to your team in a voice that all members can hear and interpret. A crisp, vigorous voice commands attention and respect; garbled and weak speech is tuned out. It's OK—in fact, appropriate—to soften your voice when speaking to a player individually about a personal problem. But most of the time your messages will be for all your players to hear, so make sure they can! An enthusiastic voice also motivates players and tells them you enjoy being their coach. A word of caution, however: don't dominate the setting with a booming voice that detracts attention from players' performances.

Sometimes what you say, even if stated loud and clear, won't sink in the first time. This may be particularly true with young cricketers hearing words they don't understand. To avoid boring repetition and yet still get your message across, say the same thing in a slightly different way. For instance, you might first tell your players 'Slide your bat'. Soon afterward, remind them 'When running between wickets, slide your bat starting just in front of the crease'. The second form of message may get through to players who missed it the first time around.

Be Consistent

People often say things in ways that imply a different message. For example, a touch of sarcasm added to the words 'way to go' sends an entirely different message than the words themselves suggest. It is essential that you avoid sending such mixed messages. Keep the tone of your voice consistent with the words you use. And don't say something one day and contradict it the next; players will get confused. If you still aren't certain whether your players understand, ask them to repeat the message back to you. As the old saying goes, 'If they can't say it, they can't play it'.

Nonverbal Messages

Just as you should be consistent in the tone of voice and words you use, you should also keep your verbal and nonverbal messages consistent. An extreme example of failing to do this would be shaking your head, indicating disapproval, while at the same time telling a player 'Nice try'. Which is the player to believe, your gesture or your words?

Messages can be sent nonverbally in a number of ways. Facial expressions and body language are just two of the more obvious forms of nonverbal signals that can help you when you coach.

Facial Expressions

The look on a person's face is the quickest clue to what he or she thinks or feels. Your players know this, so they will study your face, looking for any sign that will tell them more than the words you say. Don't try to fool them by putting on a happy or blank 'mask'. They'll see through it, and you'll lose credibility.

Serious, stone-faced expressions are no help to kids who need cues as to how they are performing. They will just assume you're unhappy or disinterested. Don't be afraid to smile. A smile from a coach can give a great boost to an unsure young player. Plus, a smile lets your players know that you are happy coaching them. But don't overdo it, or your players won't be able to tell when you are genuinely pleased by something they've done or when you are just putting on a smiling face.

Body Language

What would your players think you were feeling if you came to practice slouched over, with head down and shoulders slumped? Tired? Bored? Unhappy? What would they think you were feeling if you watched them during a game with your hands on your hips, your jaw clenched, and your face reddened? Upset with them? Disgusted at the umpire? Mad at a supporter? Probably some or all of these things would enter your players' minds. And none of these impressions is the kind you want your players to have of you. That's why you should carry yourself in a pleasant, confident, and vigorous manner. Such a posture not only projects happiness with your coaching role, but also provides a good example for your young players who may model your behaviour.

Physical contact can also be a very important use of body language. A handshake, a pat on the head or an arm around the shoulder are effective ways of showing approval, concern, affection, and joy to your players. Keep within the obvious moral and legal limits, but don't be reluctant to show your approval.

How Can I Improve My Receiving Skills?

Now, let's examine the other half of the communication process—receiving messages. Too often people are very good senders but very poor receivers of messages. As a coach of young players, it is essential that you are able to fulfil both roles effectively.

The requirements for receiving messages are quite simple, but receiving skills are perhaps less satisfying and therefore underdeveloped compared to sending skills. People seem to naturally enjoy hearing themselves talk more than others. But if you are willing to read about the keys to receiving messages and to make a strong effort to use them with your players, you'll be surprised by what you've been missing.

Attention!

First, you must pay attention; you must want to hear what others have to communicate to you. That's not always easy when you're busy coaching and have many things competing for your attention. But in one-to-one or team meetings with players, you must really focus on what they are telling you, both verbally and nonverbally. You'll be amazed at the little signals you pick up. Not only will such focused attention help you catch every word your players say, but you'll also notice your players' moods and physical states, and you'll get an idea of your players' feelings toward you and other players on the team.

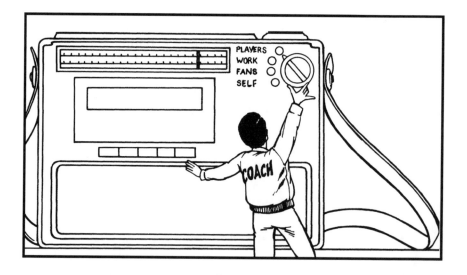

Listen CARE-FULLY

How we receive messages from others, perhaps more than anything else we do, demonstrates how much we care for the sender and what that person has to tell us. If you care little for your players or have little regard for what they have to say, it will show in how you attend and listen to them. Check yourself. Do you find your mind wandering to what you are going to do after practice while one of your players is talking to you? Do you frequently have to ask your players, 'What did you say?' If so, you need to work on your receiving mechanics of attending and listening. But perhaps the most critical question you should ask yourself, if you find that you're missing the messages your players send, is this: Do I care?

How Do I Put It All Together?

So far we've discussed separately the sending and receiving of messages. But we all know that senders and receivers switch roles several times during an interaction. One person initiates a communication by sending a message to another person, who then receives the message. The receiver then switches roles and becomes the sender by responding to the person who sent the initial message. These verbal and nonverbal responses are called feedback.

Your players will be looking to you for feedback all the time. They will want to know how you think they are performing, what you think of their ideas, and whether their efforts please you. Obviously, you can respond in many different ways. How you respond will

strongly affect your players. So let's take a look at a few general types of feedback and examine their possible effects.

Providing Instructions

With young players, much of your feedback will involve answering questions about how to play cricket. Your instructive responses to these questions should include both verbal and nonverbal feedback. Here are some suggestions for giving instructional feedback:

- Keep verbal instructions simple and concise.
- Use demonstrations to provide nonverbal instructional feedback.
- 'Walk' players through the skill, or use a slow-motion demonstration if they are having trouble learning.

Correcting Errors

When your players perform incorrectly, you need to provide informative feedback to correct the error—and the sooner the better. When you do correct errors, keep in mind these two principles: use negative criticism sparingly, and keep calm.

Use Negative Criticism Sparingly

Although you may need to punish players for horseplay or dangerous activities by scolding or removing them from activity temporarily, avoid reprimanding players for performance errors. Admonishing players for honest mistakes makes them afraid to even try. Nothing ruins a youngster's enjoyment of a sport more than a coach who harps on every mistake. So instead, correct your players by using the positive approach. Your players will enjoy playing more, and you'll enjoy coaching more.

Keep Calm

Don't fly off the handle when your players make mistakes. Remember, you're coaching young and inexperienced players, not pros.

You'll therefore see more incorrect than correct technique, and you'll probably have more discipline problems than you expect. But throwing a tantrum over each error or misbehaviour will only inhibit your players or suggest to them the wrong kind of behaviour to model. So let your players know that mistakes aren't the end of the world; stay controlled!

Giving Positive Feedback

Praising players when they have performed or behaved well is an effective way of getting them to repeat (or try to repeat) that behaviour in the future. And positive feedback for effort is an especially effective way to motivate youngsters to work on difficult skills. So rather than shouting and providing negative feedback to a player who has made a mistake, try offering players a compliment sandwich, described on page 22.

Sometimes just the way you word feedback can make it more positive than negative. For example, instead of saying, 'Don't catch the ball that way', you might say, 'Catch the ball this way'. Then your players will be focusing on what to do instead of what not to do.

You can give positive feedback verbally and nonverbally. Telling a player, especially in front of teammates, that he or she has performed well is a great way to boost the youngster's confidence. And a pat on the back or a handshake can be a very tangible way of communicating your recognition of a player's performance.

Coaches, be positive!

Only a very small percentage of ASEP-trained coaches' behaviours are negative.

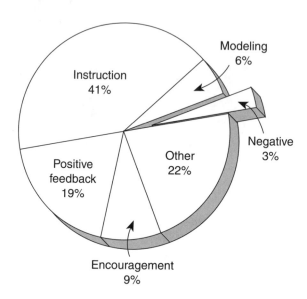

Who Else Do I Need to Communicate With?

Coaching involves not only sending and receiving messages and providing proper feedback to players, but also interacting with parents, spectators, umpires, and opposing coaches. If you don't communicate effectively with these groups of people, your coaching career will be unpleasant and short-lived. So try the following suggestions for communicating with these groups.

Parents

A player's parents need to be assured that their son or daughter is under the direction of a coach who is both knowledgeable about cricket and concerned about the youngster's well-being. You can put their worries to rest by holding a preseason parent-orientation meeting in which you describe your background and your approach to coaching.

If parents contact you with a concern during the season, listen to them closely and try to offer positive responses. If you need to communicate with parents, catch them after a practice, give them a phone call, or send a note through the mail. Messages sent to parents through children are too often lost, misinterpreted, or forgotten.

Spectators

The stands probably won't be overflowing at your games, but that only means that you'll more easily hear the few spectators who criticise your coaching. When you hear something negative said about the job you're doing, don't respond to it. Keep calm, consider whether the message has any value, and if not, forget it. Acknowledging critical, unwarranted comments from a spectator during a game will only encourage others to voice their opinions. So put away your 'rabbit ears' and communicate to spectators, through your actions, that you are a confident, competent coach.

Even if you are ready to withstand the negative comments of spectators, your players may not be. Prepare your players for spectators' criticisms. Tell them it is you, not the spectators, to whom they should listen. If you notice that one of your players is rattled by a spectator's comment, reassure the player that your evaluation is more objective and favourable—and the one that counts.

Umpires

How you communicate with umpires will have a great influence on the way your players behave toward them. Therefore, you need to set an example. Greet umpires with a handshake, an introduction, and perhaps some casual conversation about the upcoming contest. Indicate your respect for them before, during, and after the game. Don't make nasty remarks, shout, or use disrespectful body gestures. Your player will see you do it, and they'll get the idea that such behaviour is appropriate. Plus, if the official hears or sees you, the communication between the two of you will break down.

Opposing Coaches

Make an effort to meet the coach of the opposing team before the game. Perhaps the two of you can work out a special arrangement for the contest if it is necessary, such as allowing more than 11 fielders on the ground at one time. During the game, don't get into a personal feud with the opposing coach. Remember, it's the kids, not the coaches, who are competing. And by getting along well with the opposing coach, you'll show your players that competition involves cooperation.

✔ *Summary Checklist*

Now, check your coach-communication skills by answering 'Yes' or 'No' to the following questions:

	Yes	No
1. Are your verbal messages to your players positive and honest?	____	____
2. Do you speak loudly, clearly, and in a language your players understand?	____	____
3. Do you remember to repeat instructions to your players, in case they didn't hear you the first time?	____	____

	Yes	No

4. Are the tone of your voice and your nonverbal messages consistent with the words you use? _____ _____

5. Do your facial expressions and body language express interest in and happiness with your coaching role? _____ _____

6. Are you attentive to your players and able to pick up even their small verbal and nonverbal cues? _____ _____

7. Do you really care about what your players say to you? _____ _____

8. Do you instruct rather than criticise when your players make errors? _____ _____

9. Are you usually positive when responding to things your players say and do? _____ _____

10. Do you try to communicate in a cooperative and respectful manner with players' parents, spectators, umpires, and opposing coaches? _____ _____

If you answered 'No' to any of the above questions, you may want to refer back to the section of the chapter where the topic was discussed. Now is the time to address communication problems, not when you're on the field with your players.

How Do I Get My Team Ready to Play?

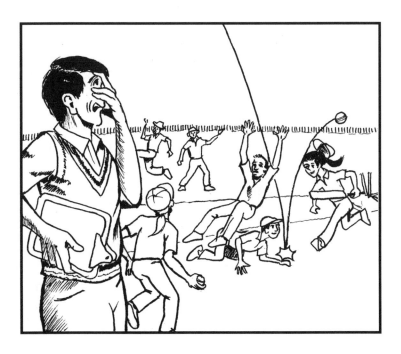

To coach cricket, you must understand the basic rules, skills, and strategies. The second part of this book provides the basic information you'll need to comprehend the sport.

But all the cricket knowledge in the world will do you little good unless you present it effectively to your players. That's why this unit is so important. Here you will learn the steps to take when teaching sport skills, as well as practical guidelines for planning your season and individual practices.

How Do I Teach Cricket Skills?

Many people believe that the only qualification needed to coach is to have played the sport. It's helpful to have played, but there is much more to coaching successfully. Even if you haven't played or even watched cricket, you can still learn to coach successfully with this IDEA:

> I — Introduce the skill.
>
> D — Demonstrate the skill.
>
> E — Explain the skill.
>
> A — Attend to players practising the skill.

Introduce the Skill

Players, especially young and inexperienced ones, need to know what skill they are learning and why they are learning it. You should therefore take these three steps every time you introduce a skill to your players:

1. Get your players' attention.
2. Name the skill.
3. Explain the importance of the skill.

Get Your Players' Attention

Because youngsters are easily distracted, use some method to get their attention. Some coaches use interesting news items or stories. Others use jokes. And others simply project enthusiasm that gets their players to listen. Whatever method you use, speak slightly above the normal volume and look your players in the eyes when you speak.

Also, position the players so they can see and hear you. Arrange the players in two or three evenly spaced rows, facing you and not the sun or some source of distraction. Then ask if everyone can see and hear you before you begin.

Name the Skill

Although you might mention other common names for the skill, decide which one you'll use and stick with it. This will help avoid confusion and enhance communication among your players. For example, refer to the preparatory throwing position as the 'goose neck' position as the term for the appropriate skill and use it consistently.

Explain the Importance of the Skill

Although the importance of a skill may be apparent to you, your players may be less able to see how the skill will help them become better cricketers. Offer them a reason for learning the skill and describe how the skill relates to more advanced skills.

> 'The most difficult aspect of coaching is this: coaches must learn to let athletes learn. Sport skills should be taught so they have meaning to the child, not just meaning to the coach.'
>
> Rainer Martens, ASEP Founder

Demonstrate the Skill

The demonstration step is the most important part of teaching a cricket skill to young players who may have never done anything closely resembling it. They need a picture, not just words. They need to see how the skill is performed.

If you are unable to perform the skill correctly, have an assistant coach or someone skilled in cricket perform the demonstration. A young representative player would be an excellent choice. These tips will help make your demonstrations more effective:

- Use correct form.
- Demonstrate the skill several times.
- Slow down the skill, if possible, during one or two performances so players can see every movement involved.
- Perform the skill at different angles so your players can get a full perspective of it.
- Demonstrate the skill from both sides of the body.
- Demonstrate the skill slowly. Then demonstrate the skill at normal speed.

Explain the Skill

Players learn more effectively when they're given a brief explanation of the skill along with the demonstration. Use simple terms to describe the skill and, if possible, relate it to previously learned skills. Ask your players whether they understand your description. A good technique is to ask the team to repeat your explanation. Ask ques-

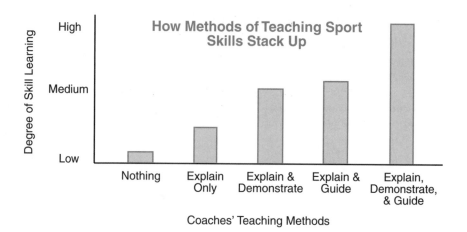

tions such as 'What are you going to do first?' 'Then what?' Watch for looks of confusion or uncertainty and repeat your explanation and demonstration of those points. If possible, use different words so that your players get a chance to try to understand from a different perspective.

Complex skills often are better understood when they are explained in more manageable parts. For instance, if you want to teach your players how to field ground balls, close to the wicket, you might take the following steps:

- Show them a correct performance of the entire skill and explain its function.
- Break down the skill and point out its component parts to your players.
- Have players perform each of the component skills you have already taught them, such as getting into the ready position, sliding or charging to meet the ball, watching it into the hands, stopping, pivoting, and throwing to the appropriate end.
- After players have demonstrated their ability to perform the separate parts of the skill in sequence, reexplain the entire skill.
- Have players practise the skill.

One caution: Young players have short attention spans, and a long demonstration or explanation of the skill will bore them. So spend no more than a few minutes combined on the introduction, demonstration, and explanation phases. Then get the players active in attempts to perform the skill. The total IDEA should be completed in 10 minutes or less, followed by individual and group practice activities.

Attend to Players Practising the Skill

If the skill you selected was within your players' capabilities, and you have done an effective job of introducing, demonstrating, and explaining it, your players should be ready to attempt the skill. Some players may need to be physically guided through the movements during their first few attempts. For example, some players may need your hands-on help to hold their wrists and rotate their arms properly on their initial bowling attempts. Walking unsure players through the skill in this way will help them gain confidence to perform the skill on their own.

Your teaching duties don't end when all your players have demonstrated that they understand how to perform the skill. In fact, a significant part of your teaching will involve observing closely the hit-and-miss trial performances of your players.

As you observe players' efforts in drills and activities, offer positive, corrective feedback in the form of the 'compliment sandwich' described in unit 3. If a player performs the skill properly, acknowledge it and offer praise. Keep in mind that your feedback will have a great influence on your players' motivation to practise and improve their performance.

Remember, too, that young players need individual instruction. So set aside a time before, during, or after practice to give individual help.

What Planning Do I Need to Do?

Beginning coaches often make the mistake of showing up for the first practice with no particular plan in mind. These coaches find that their practices are not organised, their players are frustrated and inattentive, and the amount and quality of their skill instruction is limited. Planning is essential to successful teaching and coaching. And it doesn't begin on the way to practice!

Preseason Planning

Effective coaches begin planning well before the start of the season. Among the preseason measures that will make the season more enjoyable, successful, and safe for you and your players are the following:

- Familiarise yourself with the sport organisation you are involved in, especially its philosophy and rules regarding junior cricket.
- Examine the availability of facilities, equipment, instructional aids, and other materials needed for practices and games.

- Find out what fund-raising you and your players will be expected to do, and decide on the best way to meet your goals.
- Make arrangements for any team travel that will be required during the season. Consider clearance forms, supervision, transportation, equipment, contacting parents, and safety.
- Check to see whether you have adequate liability insurance to cover you when one of your players gets hurt (see unit 5). If you don't, get some. Gaining coaching accreditation will help!
- Establish your coaching priorities regarding having fun, developing players' skills, and winning.
- Select and meet with your assistant coaches to discuss the philosophy, goals, team rules, and plans for the season.
- Register players for the team. Have them complete a player information form and obtain medical clearance forms, if required.
- Institute an injury-prevention program for your players.
- Adopt a SunSmart policy (contact your State or Territory Cricket Association for further information).
- Hold an orientation meeting to inform parents of your background, philosophy, goals, and instructional approach. Also, give a brief overview of the association's rules, terms, and strategies to familiarise parents or guardians with the sport.

You may be surprised at the number of things you should do even before the first practice. But if you address them during the pre-season, the season will be much more enjoyable and productive for you and your players.

In-Season Planning

Your choice of activities during the season should be based on whether they will help your players develop physical and mental skills, knowledge of rules and game tactics, sportsmanship, and love for the sport. All of these goals are important, but we'll focus on the skills and tactics of cricket to give you an idea of how to itemise your objectives.

Goal Setting

What you plan to do during the season must be reasonable for the maturity and skill level of your players. In terms of cricket skills and tactics, you should teach young players the basics and move on to more complex activities only after the players have mastered these easier techniques and strategies.

To begin the season, your instructional goals might include the following:

- Players will be able to be prepared in the field.
- Players will be able to assume an effective stance when batting, when the ball is bowled.
- Players who bowl will be able to grip the ball for proper release.
- Players will be able to throw the ball to a target.
- Players will be able to use proper mechanics when catching the ball.
- Players will demonstrate knowledge of cricket rules.
- Players will demonstrate knowledge of basic attacking and defensive strategies.
- Players will be able to communicate with teammates.
- Players will develop a respect for teamwork.

- Players will play hard and have fun at the same time.
- Players will show respect for umpires, coaches, and other players.
- Players will learn how to win with class and how to lose with grace.

Organising

After you've defined the skills and tactics you want your players to learn during the season, you can plan how to teach them to your players in practices. But be flexible! If your players are having difficulty learning a skill or tactic, take some extra time until they get the hang of it—even if that means moving back your schedule. After all, if your players are unable to perform the fundamental skills, they'll never execute the more complex skills you have scheduled for them, and they won't have much fun trying. Still, it helps to have a plan for progressing players through skills during the season.

The way you organise your season may also help your players to develop socially and psychologically. By giving your players responsibility for certain aspects of practices—leading warm-up and stretching activities are common examples—you help players to develop self-esteem and take responsibility for themselves and the team. As you plan your season, consider ways to provide your players with experiences that lead them to steadily improve these skills.

What Makes Up a Good Practice?

A good instructional plan makes practice preparation much easier. Have players work on more important and less difficult goals in early-season practice sessions. And see to it that players master basic skills before moving on to more advanced ones.

It is helpful to establish one goal for each practice, but try to include a variety of activities related to that goal. For example, although your primary objective might be to improve players' front foot driving skill, you should have players perform several different drills designed to enhance that single skill. To add more variety to your practices, vary the order of the activities you schedule for players to perform.

In general, we recommend that in each of your practices you do the following:

- Warm up.
- Practise previously taught skills.
- Teach and practise new skills.
- Practise under competitive conditions.
- Cool down.
- Evaluate.

Warm Up

As you're checking the roster and announcing the performance goals for the practice, your players should be preparing their bodies for vigorous activity. A 5- to 10-minute period of easy-paced activities (three-quarter-speed running around the field), stretching, and callisthenics should be sufficient for youngsters to limber their muscles and reduce the risk of injury.

Practise Previously Taught Skills

Devote part of each practice to having players work on the fundamental skills they already know. But remember, kids like variety. Thus you should organise and modify drills so that everyone is involved and stays interested. Praise and encourage players when you notice improvement, and offer individual assistance to those who need help.

Teach and Practise New Skills

Gradually build on your players' existing skills by giving players something new to practise each session. The proper method for teaching sport skills is described on pages 36–40. Refer to those pages if you have any questions about teaching new skills or if you want to evaluate your teaching approach periodically during the season. Players should be given plenty of practice at a skill before using it in a competitive situation.

Practise Under Competitive Conditions

Competition among teammates during practices prepares players for actual games and informs young athletes about their abilities relative to their peers. Youngsters also seem to have more fun in competitive activities.

You can create gamelike conditions by using competitive drills and modified games (see units 6 and 7). However, consider the following guidelines before introducing competition into your practices:

- All players should have an equal opportunity to participate.
- Match players by ability and physical maturity.
- Make sure that players can execute fundamental skills before they compete in groups.
- Emphasise performing well, not winning, in every competition.
- Give players room to make mistakes by avoiding constant evaluation of their performances.

Cool Down

Each practice should wind down with a 5- to 10-minute period of light exercise, including jogging, performance of simple skills, and some stretching. The cool-down allows athlete's bodies to return to

the resting state and avoid stiffness, and it affords you an opportunity to review the practice.

Evaluate

At the end of practice spend a few minutes with your players reviewing how well the session accomplished the goals you had set. Even if your evaluation is negative, show optimism for future practices and send players off on an upbeat note.

How Do I Put a Practice Together?

Simply knowing the six practice components is not enough. You must also be able to arrange those components into a logical progression and fit them into a time schedule. Now, using your instructional goals as a guide for selecting what skills to have your players work on, try to plan several cricket practices you might conduct. The following example should help you get started.

Sample Practice Plan		
Component	**Time**	**Activity or drill**
Warm-up	10 min	Warm-up game such as Snowball Tag
		In pairs throwing the ball to each other over various distances
Practise previously taught skills	20 min	Catching fly balls—individually throwing ball in the air to self—using correct techniques
		Group drill—coach hitting fly balls
Teach and practise new skills	20 min	Front foot drives: from batting tees into net and from rolled balls rolled down by partner

(continued)

Sample Practice Plan *(continued)*		
Component	**Time**	**Activity or drill**
Practise under competitive conditions	30 min	Minor game—two teams (one batting, the other fielding)
		Coach throws the ball for the batter to drive
		Fielders attempt to trap the ball and execute a run out
Cool-down and evaluation	10 min	Easy throwing
		Stretching
		Quick review (for next practice or game)

✔ *Summary Checklist*

During your cricket season, check your planning and teaching skills periodically. As you gain more coaching experience, you should be able to answer 'Yes' to each of the following.

When you plan, do you remember to plan for	Yes	No
1. preseason events such as player registration, fund-raising, travel, liability protection, use of facilities, and parent orientation?	____	____
2. season goals such as the development of players' physical skills, mental skills, sportsmanship, and enjoyment?	____	____
3. practice components such as warm-up, practising previously taught skills, teaching and practising new skills, practising under competitive conditions, cool-down, and evaluation?	____	____

When you teach cricket skills to your players, do you

	Yes	No
1. arrange the players so all can see and hear?	___	___
2. introduce the skill clearly and explain its importance?	___	___
3. demonstrate the skill properly several times?	___	___
4. explain the skill simply and accurately?	___	___
5. attend closely to players practising the skill?	___	___
6. offer corrective, positive feedback or praise after observing players' attempts at the skill?	___	___

What About Safety?

One of your players takes off for a single and in trying to avoid being hit by the incoming ball deviates and collides with the bowler. Although he has avoided being run out, he is not getting up and seems to be in pain. What do you do?

No coach wants to see players get hurt. But injury remains a reality of sport participation; consequently, you must be prepared to provide first aid when injuries occur and to protect yourself against unjustified lawsuits. Fortunately, coaches can institute many preventive measures to reduce the risk. This unit will describe how you can

- create the safest possible environment for your players,
- provide emergency first aid to players when they get hurt, and
- protect yourself from injury liability.

How Do I Keep My Players From Getting Hurt?

Poor preventive measures can lead to injuries. Part of your planning, described in unit 4, should include steps that give your players the best possible chance for injury-free participation. These steps include the following:

- Preseason physical examination
- Good nutrition
- Physical conditioning
- Equipment and facilities inspection
- Matching athletes by physical maturity
- Warning players of inherent risks
- Proper supervision and record keeping
- Fitness
- Warm-up and cool-down
- Water breaks

Preseason Physical Examination

In the absence of severe injury or ongoing illness, your players should have a physical examination every two years. Any player with a known complication must obtain a physician's consent before participation is allowed. You should also have players' parents or guardians sign a participation agreement form and a release form to allow their children to be treated in case of an emergency.

INFORMED CONSENT FORM

I hereby give my permission for _____ to participate

in _____ during the cricket season beginning in _____.
Further, I authorise the club to provide emergency treatment of an injury to or illness of my child if qualified medical personnel consider treatment necessary and perform the treatment. This authorisation is granted only if I cannot be reached and reasonable effort has been made to reach me.

Date _____   Parent or guardian _____

Address _____   Phone (___) _____

Family physician _____   Phone (___) _____

Pre-existing medical conditions (e.g., allergies or chronic illnesses) _____

_____

Other(s) to also contact in case of emergency _____

_____

Relationship to child _____   Phone (___) _____

My child and I are aware that participating in _____
is a potentially hazardous activity. I assume all risks associated with participation in this sport, including but not limited to falls, contact with other participants, the effects of the weather, traffic, and other reasonable-risk conditions associated with the sport. All such risks to my child are known and understood by me.

I understand this informed consent form and agree to its conditions on behalf of my child.

Child's signature _____   Date _____

Parent's signature _____   Date _____

Nutrition

Increasingly, disordered eating and unhealthy dietary habits are affecting young athletes. Let players and parents know the importance of healthy eating and the dangers that can arise from efforts to lose weight too quickly. Young cricket players need to supply their bodies with the extra energy they need to keep up with the demands of practices and games. Ask your state cricket association about information that you can pass on to your players and their parents, and include a discussion of basic, commonsense nutrition in your parent-orientation meeting.

Physical Conditioning

Muscles, tendons, and ligaments unaccustomed to vigorous and long-lasting physical activity are prone to injury. Therefore, prepare your athletes to withstand the exertion of playing cricket. An effective conditioning program for cricket involves running, throwing, and bowling.

Make conditioning drills and activities fun. Include a skill component, such as running between wickets, to prevent players from becoming bored or viewing the activity as work.

Keep in mind, too, that players on your team may respond differently to conditioning activities. Wide-ranging levels of fitness or natural ability might mean that an activity that challenges one child is beyond another's ability to complete safely. The environment may also affect players' responses to activity. The same workout that is effective on a cool morning might be hazardous to players on a hot, humid afternoon. Similarly, an activity children excel in at sea level might present a risk at higher altitudes. An ideal conditioning program prepares players for the sport's demands without neglecting physical and environmental factors that affect their safety.

Equipment and Facilities Inspection

Another way to prevent injury is to check the quality and fit of the clothes and protective equipment your players use. Slick-soled, poor-fitting, or unlaced cricket shoes; unstrapped eyeglasses; and jewellery are dangerous on the cricket field. Specify to players what they should wear—such as well-soled shoes that are essential for good footing. Inspect the equipment before you distribute it, after you have assigned it to the players, and regularly during the season. Check to see that grids on helmets are secure and well spaced.

Remember also to examine regularly the field and nets on which your players practise and play. Remove hazards, report conditions you cannot remedy, and request maintenance as necessary. If unsafe conditions exist, either make adaptations to avoid risk to your players' safety or stop the practice or game until safe conditions have been restored.

Matching Athletes by Maturity and Warning of Inherent Risks

Children of the same age may differ in height and weight by up to 15 cm and 25 kg. In cricket, size is less of an advantage than in some other sports. Yet it is hardly fair to pit an underdeveloped young athlete against a tall, strong, fast bowler. Try to give smaller, less mature children a better chance to succeed and avoid injury, and larger children more of a challenge. Experience, ability, and emotional maturity are additional factors to keep in mind when matching players on the field.

Matching helps protect you from certain liability concerns. But you must also warn players of the inherent risks involved in playing

cricket because 'failure to warn' is one of the most successful arguments employed in lawsuits against coaches. So thoroughly explain the inherent risks of cricket and make sure each player knows, understands, and appreciates those risks.

The preseason parent-orientation meeting is a good opportunity to explain the risks of cricket to parents and players. It is also a good time to have both the players and their parents sign waivers releasing you from liability should an injury occur. Such waivers do not relieve you of responsibility for your players' well-being, but lawyers recommend having them.

Proper Supervision and Record Keeping

When you work with youngsters, your mere presence in the area of play is not enough; you must actively plan and direct team activities and closely observe and evaluate players' participation. You're the watchdog responsible for the players' well-being. So if you notice a player limping or grimacing, give him or her a rest and examine the extent of the injury.

As a coach, you're also required to enforce the rules of the sport, prohibit dangerous horseplay, and hold practices only under safe weather conditions. These specific supervisory activities will make the play environment safer for your players and will help protect you from liability if a mishap does occur.

For further liability protection, keep records of your season plans, practice plans, and players' injuries. Season and practice plans come in handy when you need evidence that players have been taught certain skills, and accurate, detailed accident report forms offer protection against unfounded lawsuits. Ask for these forms from the organisation to which you belong. Hold onto these records for several years so that a former player's 'old cricket injury' doesn't come back to haunt you.

Fitness

Skill and mental application are critical ingredients for every cricketer. Fitness, too, makes an important contribution to both individual and team performance. Remember the old adage that skill performance decreases with fatigue. Therefore, the fitter the individual, the longer he or she can perform at an *optimum* level and the better chance the individual has to prevent injury.

Warm-Up

Warm-up is a vital part of any competition or strenuous exercise session. It results in improved flexibility and prepares the participant's mind, heart, muscles, and joints, thus reducing the likelihood of injury.

The warm-up should include 5 to 10 minutes of general activity before the stretching session.

Stretching

Stretching, before and after activity, is another vital factor in the prevention of injury. Without stretching, muscles lose their flexibility and may fail to respond when they are used, possibly resulting in injury.

> *Back flexion* — Lie on your back. Pull both knees to your chest (see figure 5.1). Hold for 10 seconds. Rock back and forth with your chin tucked into your chest.

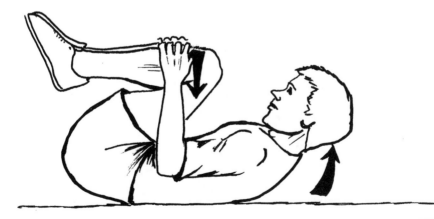

Figure 5.1 The back flexion stretch.

Hip flexion (hamstring) — Lie on your back, holding the right leg with the hands as shown in figure 5.2. Keep the opposite knee bent. Straighten the knee as far as you can. Hold for 10 seconds, then do the same with the left leg.

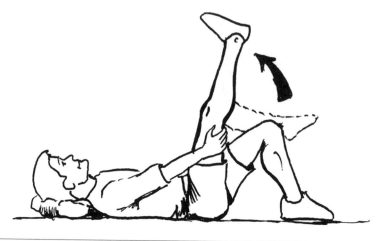

Figure 5.2   The hip flexion (hamstring) stretch.

Hip flexion — Lie on your back. Pull the right knee up toward the chest as far as you can (see figure 5.3). Hold for 10 seconds, then do the same with the left leg.

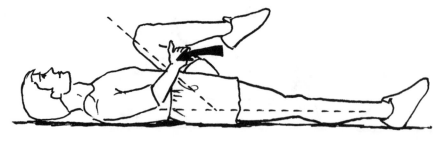

Figure 5.3   The hip flexion stretch.

Back rotation — Lie on your back with knees bent and feet together, arms out to the sides. Bring the knees near the chest as shown in figure 5.4. Rotate the knees to the right as you turn your head in the opposite direction, until you feel a stretch. Hold for 5 seconds, then drop knees to the left. Repeat this several times, rotating knees from left to right.

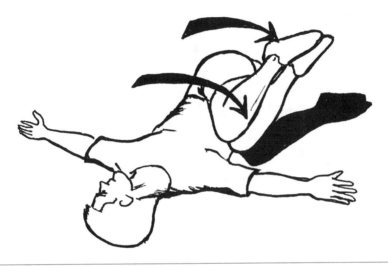

Figure 5.4 The back rotation stretch.

Hip abduction — Sit with your knees bent, feet together, as shown in figure 5.5. Hold the ankles and bring heels close to groin. Press the knees down toward the floor, leaning forward and pressing with your elbows as shown. Hold for 10 seconds.

Figure 5.5 The hip abduction stretch.

Pelvic rotation — Assume the position shown in figure 5.6, with the left leg straight. Press the pelvis down toward the floor as shown. Hold for 10 seconds, then do the same with the right leg straight.

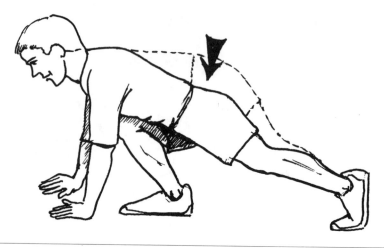

Figure 5.6 The pelvic rotation stretch.

Shoulder and triceps stretch — Place right hand over shoulder and onto back with elbow next to right ear. Place left hand on top of right elbow and pull backwards to obtain a stretch (see figure 5.7). Hold for 10 seconds and then repeat with opposite arm.

Figure 5.7 The shoulder and triceps stretch.

Pectoral stretch — Link hands behind the back with palms up. Push hands down and then back away from the body, as in figure 5.8, until you feel a stretch in the chest muscles. Hold for 10 seconds.

Figure 5.8 The pectoral stretch.

Deltoid stretch — Place your right arm across the body and over the left shoulder. Hold the right elbow with the left hand, pulling the right upper arm into the chest (see figure 5.9). Hold for 10 seconds when you feel a stretch in the area of the upper arm and across the shoulder where both connect. Switch arms and repeat.

Figure 5.9 The deltoid stretch.

Stretching rules
- Warm up before stretching.
- Stretch before and after exercise.
- Stretch alternative muscle groups (e.g., triceps then biceps or quadriceps then hamstrings).
- Stretch gently and slowly.
- Never bounce or stretch rapidly.
- Stretch to the point of tension or discomfort, but never to the point of pain.
- Don't hold your breath when stretching; breathing should be slow and easy.

Cool-Down

Cool-downs are important because they prevent the pooling of blood in the limbs, which could lead to fainting or dizziness. They also improve the recovery of the heart, muscles, and other tissues after exercise.

An effective cool-down consists of a gradual reduction in activity levels for 5 to 10 minutes followed by a comprehensive stretching programme.

Fluid Replacement

Cricket is a summer sport often played in very warm conditions. With this in mind, the coach should seriously consider and account for the following points:

- Thirst is a poor indicator of the need for fluid replacement—therefore, athletes must drink before they are thirsty.
- Plain water is best for fluid replacement (fruit juice and sport drinks are also acceptable).
- The average person requires 6 to 8 glasses of water a day. During training, this need can increase to up to 12 glasses a day (fruit juice or small amounts of cordial can be added for taste).

- The loss of body fluids can cause fatigue or muscle cramps and decreases an athlete's performance.
- During heavy exercise in moderate temperatures (22° C), 2 to 3 L of sweat can be lost every hour. Only half this amount can be replaced during exercise.
- If as little as 2 percent of body weight is lost via dehydration, exercise performance will be impaired.
- Further fluid loss will compromise health.
- Adequate hydration allows a person to perform at his or her best by maximising the flow of oxygen and nutrients to the muscle cells. (Reference: *B.V.C.A Bolters Manual.*)

What If One of My Players Gets Hurt?

Though no one expects a coach to be a medical specialist, understanding fundamental first aid is part of a good coach's responsibility. Figures 5.10 and 5.11 (see pages 64 and 65) provide procedural guidelines in assessing the immediate management of injuries.

How Do I Protect Myself?

When one of your players is injured, naturally your first concern is his or her well-being. Your feelings for children, after all, are what made you decide to coach. Unfortunately, you must consider something else as well: can you be held liable for the injury?

From a legal standpoint, a coach has nine duties to fulfil. We've discussed all but planning (see unit 4) in this unit:

1. Provide a safe environment.
2. Properly plan the activity.
3. Provide adequate and proper equipment.
4. Match athletes by size and ability level.
5. Warn players and their parents of inherent risks in the sport.
6. Supervise the action closely.

Initial action

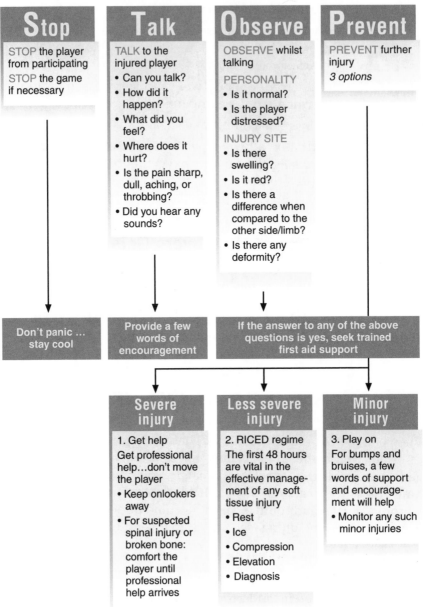

Figure 5.10 Initial action STOP table.

	HOW	WHY
Rest the injured part	Movement of injured part only when pain is absent	Activity would promote bleeding by increasing blood flow
Ice	**The conventional methods are:** • Crushed ice in a wet towelling bag • Immersion in icy water • Cold water from the tap is better than nothing • **Apply for 20 minutes every 2-3 hours for the first 48 hours** **Caution:** • Do not apply ice directly to skin as ice burns can occur • Do not apply to people with circulatory problems • **Children have a lower tolerance to ice**	• Reduces inflammatory response • Reduces pain • Reduces muscle spasm
Compression	Apply a firm wide bandage over a large area covering the injured part	• Reduces bleeding and swelling • Provides support for the injured part
Elevation	Raise injured area above the level of the heart at all possible times	• Reduces bleeding and swelling • Reduces pain
Diagnosis	Refer to a suitably qualified professional such as a doctor or physiotherapist	• To ascertain the extent of the injury • To gain other expert advice on the rehabilitation program required

Figure 5.11 The RICED method.

7. Evaluate athletes for injury or incapacitation.
8. Know emergency procedures and first aid.
9. Keep adequate records.

In addition to fulfilling these nine legal duties, you should check your insurance coverage to make sure your policy protects you from liability.

Summary Self-Test

Now that you've learned how to make your coaching experience safe for your players and yourself, test your knowledge of the material by answering these questions:

1. What are 10 injury-prevention measures you can institute to try to keep your players from getting hurt?
2. What are the rules for stretching?
3. What are the STOP and RICED methods?
4. What are the nine legal duties of a coach?

What Is Cricket All About?

Australia's most popular sport sees millions of cricket enthusiasts both supporting the national team's fortunes and participating in weekend cricket matches throughout the country on summer weekends. This love of cricket is shared by millions of other spectators in England, South Africa, the West Indies, New Zealand, Pakistan, India, Sri Lanka, Zimbabwe, Bangladesh, and other pockets of Europe, Canada, and Asia.

For cricket players and coaches, however, it's not simply a matter of a 'romp in the park'. This may surprise you if you are a beginning coach. But if you've coached cricket before, you realise there is more to it than just bringing the gear and filling out the team sheet.

Whether you're a first-time junior cricket coach or a seasoned veteran, you are probably interested in teaching the game effectively to young players. Units 6, 7, and 8 of *Coaching Youth Cricket* provide the basics that you need to do the job. Included are the basic rules, minor games, skills, and drills that you and your players should know.

Coaching Youth Cricket

So why take the time and trouble to coach cricket? Perhaps the best reason is that kids love the sport; give them a set of wickets, a bat, and a ball and they'll play till it's too dark to see.

Cricket fact

More than 300,000 club players register annually. This includes both senior and junior players playing in organised competitions.

Kids' fondness for the game is both a plus and a minus when it comes to coaching them. On the plus side, their interest and previous cricket experience often make them eager students of the game. On the minus side, because they have watched their heroes on TV, they may think they know more than they really do about the skills required to play cricket. So don't be shocked when one of your players allows the ball to roll through his or her legs for four whilst trying to pick it up one-handed on the boundary; that's part of the learning process and part of coaching.

But what a great opportunity! Coaching cricket gives you a chance to share with kids your knowledge and love of the game. When a player you taught to swing the ball gets his or her first wicket, you'll be hooked.

Your challenge as a junior cricket coach is to instruct your players well in the fundamentals of cricket and to keep their interest while still allowing them to have fun. To meet this challenge, read the rest of this book and then take your players to the PARK:

> P—Prepare to teach proper fundamental skill development.
>
> A—Always instill good sportsmanship and respect for the rules.
>
> R—Repeat instructions as a key to good teaching.
>
> K—Keep it fun!

What Are the Rules?

Cricket rules vary for different age groups and in different environments. For example, a 35–40 over game for U14s on a Saturday morning would often be inappropriate for a school sports session of a shorter duration.

Simple modified games such as Pairs Cricket, Double Chance, and Kanga Cricket are more suitable for middle to upper primary school children, advancing to secondary Super 8s (postprimary) and less modified versions of the traditional game played in local cricket associations.

Modified Games

In the following pages of this unit, we outline a number of modified games. These games incorporate all or most of the basic skills of batting, bowling, fielding, and wicket keeping. By including these games in your training sessions, you are giving your players an opportunity not only to practise those skills but also to have some variety and fun.

The games are listed from simple to more complex. With a little imagination, you will be able to make changes to best adapt them to your own situation. Each game is a player-centred activity, focusing on skill development, strategies, or game sense; knowledge of the rules; and general attitudinal values. For example, Pairs Cricket promotes cooperation between players.

DOUBLE CHANCE (SUITABLE FOR AGES 7–10)

Number of players.   6, 8, or 10, with players in pairs

Equipment.   2 tees, 4 markers, 3 balls, 2 bats, and 2 sets of stumps per game

All players take turns at batting, bowling, wicket keeping, and fielding. Players bat in pairs, and they can be out in three ways:

1.   Bowled—if the ball hits the wicket or base
2.   Caught—if the ball is caught by any of the fielders before it hits the ground
3.   Run out—if the batter doesn't reach 'safe ground'; that is, the crease or base indicated by the markers (see figure 6.1)

    (*No leg before wicket.)

If the batters go out they simply swap ends. They do not stop batting (until they retire). After two over (6 balls per over; therefore 12 balls per pair), the batting pair retire and the next numbered pair then have their turn to bat.

The first player bowls one over of six balls while his or her partner wicket keeps behind the batter's stumps. After the first player has completed the over, the partners swap places, and the player that was bowling now wicket keeps, and the partner bowls. Bowlers can bowl overarm or underarm.

If a pair are not batting, bowling, or wicket keeping, they are fielding, so no time is spent doing nothing. When batting, the batters can hit the ball off the tee if they miss the bowled ball as long as the bowled ball does not hit the stumps (i.e., out bowled) and on the condition that the batter has *tried* to hit the delivery bowled to him or her. The ball on the tee must be hit *in front* of the wicket, not behind or backward, for safety reasons. A batter can have only one swing at the tee ball. The ball hit is the ball in play. The idea of the game is to score as many runs as possible, but it is not 'tippity run'.

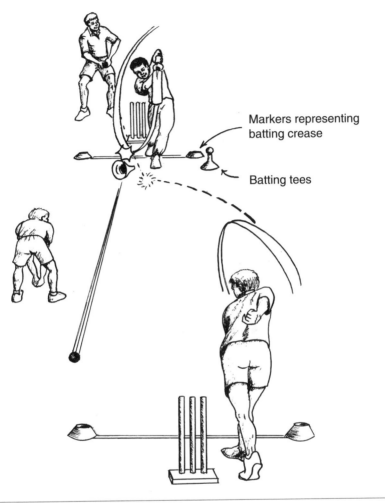

Markers representing batting crease

Batting tees

Figure 6.1   Double Chance pairs game.

PAIRS CRICKET (SUITABLE FOR AGES 10–12)

The game format and the rules are the same as in Double Chance. However, this game is played without batting tees. 'No balls' and 'wides' can be either ignored or rebowled, or the batter receives a free hit the next delivery. A free hit means that the batter can't be bowled or caught out, but only run out. As a variation to the game, players can add points to their batting score by taking catches or being involved in running out batters, for example, five bonus points for a catch or a run out. If more than one player assists in a run out, then all fielders to handle the ball receive five bonus points.

If more than one game is being conducted at the same time, players can catch any player out from any game or assist in a run out irrespective of which game the ball has come from. In other words, fielders can field for more than one game at a time. See figure 6.2.

Figure 6.2 Pairs Cricket.

DIAMOND CRICKET (SUITABLE FOR AGES 9 AND UP)

Number of players.   2 or 3 teams of 4–6 players each

Equipment.   2 bats, 1 ball, 1 marker per base, and 4 sets of stumps

The game is played around a square with stumps (or bases) at each corner, 15–20 m apart, as in baseball. (If sides have five players, you can have five bases.) Each base is occupied by a player from the batting team as well as a player from the fielding team who acts as wicket keeper and bowler. Players are assigned the numbers 1 through the number of players on the team; for example, the four players on team A are numbered 1, 2, 3, and 4, and the same for teams B and C.

The ball is bowled from one designated end (or base) only. Player 1 from team A commences bowling and the batter at the other end endeavours to hit the ball. If the batter is successful, all players on the batting team advance anticlockwise as many bases as possible. The lead batter counts the score, for example, one run for every base reached. See figure 6.3.

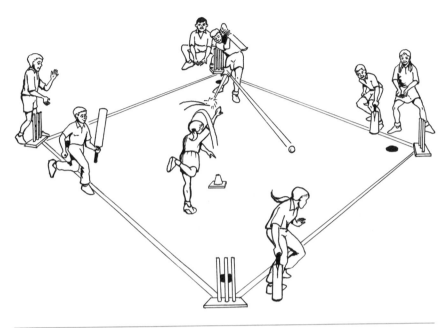

Figure 6.3   Diamond Cricket.

Should batters be out bowled or hit wicket, they simply advance one base but do not add to their score. Should a run out be completed, then no runs are scored for that hit. The batting team continue to bat until all members of the bowling team have had their turns to bowl. After player 1 from the bowling team has bowled six deliveries, the whole bowling team rotate in an anticlockwise direction, therefore bringing player 2 to the bowling crease. When all players from team A have bowled, then they take their turns at batting. Batters carry their bats at all times. The team that scores the most runs wins.

Variation.   Three Teams

Team A bat, team B bowl, and team C field. After all of team B have bowled, teams rotate: team B bat, team C bowl, team A field, and so on.

KANGA 8s

Equipment.   Bats (optional wooden or plastic) and Kanga balls. Wooden bats may be used, but it is strongly recommended that fielding restrictions be applied. It is strongly recommended that the wicket keeper wear a helmet with a visor or grill.

Members of the bowling team bowl from one end only.

All runs and extras are scored according to the accepted laws of cricket with the following exceptions:

- A ball that bounces over shoulder height while the batter is in a normal batting stance shall be deemed a 'no ball'. In addition to this, any ball that is above waist height on the FULL shall also be deemed a 'no ball'.

- Any 'no ball' shall result in a 'free hit' from the batting tee. Any 'wide ball' shall be called a 'no ball'.

- The 'free hit' must be hit from the tee in front of the square on the off side (i.e., the side in front of the batter whilst in a batting stance). The ball cannot be hit behind the wicket.

- The batter cannot be out bowled, caught, stumped, or hit wicket from a free hit but they can still be run out.

- Two lines or markers are placed at 90 degrees 60–70 cm from the line of the middle stump at the batsmen's end (see figure 6.4). In the case of a free hit, the fielding team must assume the positions they were in at the moment the delivery was made.

- Any ball that bounces more than once or rolls along the ground is deemed a fair delivery, unless the bowler is deliberately rolling it along the ground to obviously gain an advantage. The umpire may decide to *rebowl* deliveries if considered accidently unfair.

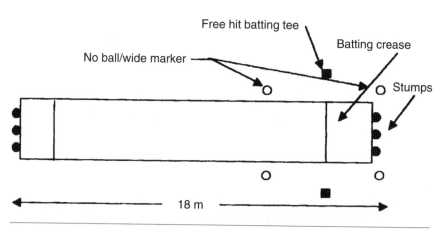

Figure 6.4 Kanga 8s straight hit.

At the moment of delivery, no players may field closer than 10 m from the bat (except behind point where gully and orthodox slips may be employed; see figures 6.5 and 6.6).

Rules pertaining to batting and outs:

- Players bat and bowl in pairs.
- Players remain batting irrespective of the number of times they are dismissed, until they have been 'in' for two overs.
- Outs can be obtained in the following ways only: bowled, caught, run out, hit wicket, or stumped.
- The only penalty for being caught is that players swap ends (this does not apply to run outs).

Boundaries regarding scoring (see figure 6.6). Variations to the scoring norm will be as follows:

- A ball hit over the boundary, other than in the 'Double Zone', on the full, scores 6 runs. If a batter chooses to hit a delivery (and connects) that would otherwise be deemed a 'no ball', they score 2 plus whatever runs are scored from the shot; however, they forfeit their free hit. If the batter chooses to leave or misses a delivery that is deemed a 'no ball', the team scores 2 runs for the 'no ball' and whatever runs they score from the free hit off the tee.
- A ball hit over the boundary, other than in the 'Double Zone', along the ground scores 4 runs (except for a free tee hit).

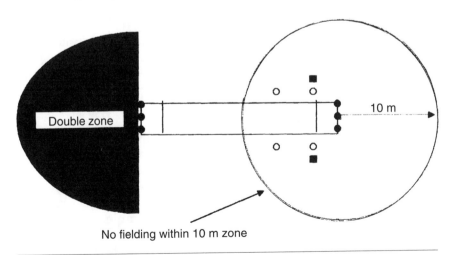

Figure 6.5 No fielding zone.

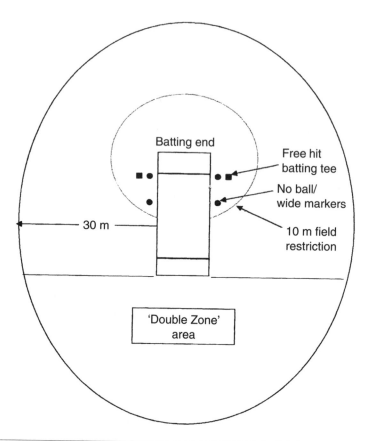

Figure 6.6   Cricket boundaries.

- If the ball is hit in the 'Double Zone', all scores are doubled. If a ball is hit to the boundary, along the ground, then 8 runs shall be accredited to the batter. If hit over the boundary on the full, then 12 runs shall be scored. If a boundary is hit from a free hit, then add 2 runs (i.e., 10 runs or 14 runs).

In the case of a free hit, the fielding team must assume the positions they were in at the moment the delivery was bowled.

Scoring.   Figure 6.7 shows a sample scoresheet. Scores will be calculated by adding 5 runs for each wicket taken onto the total number of runs your team has made. For example:

Bentleigh Primary School scored 90 runs and took 2 wickets.
Bentleigh's score: 90 + (2 × 5) = 100

KANGA 8s
SCORESHEET

_____ VS _____

☆ **MARK WICKET TAKEN WITH AN X**
☆ **MARK "WIDES" AND "NO BALLS" WITH A CIRCLE EG. ∅ + ANY RUNS SCORED**
☆ **"WIDES", "NO BALLS" RESULTS IN A "FREE HIT" OF THE TEE = 2 RUNS PLUS ANY SCORED**
☆ **RUNS ACCRUED FROM HITS INTO THE "DOUBLE ZONE" ARE DOUBLED**
☆ **BONUS POINTS = 5 RUNS PER WICKET TAKEN, ADDED TO THE BATTING TOTAL**

BATTING TEAM NAME: _____ **Primary School**

BATS	BALLS BOWLED – SCORE PER								PROGRESSIVE	
Pair No:	1	2	3	4	5	6	RUNS	WICKET	RUNS	WICKETS
PAIR 1										
PAIR 2										
PAIR 3										
PAIR 4										

INNINGS – RUNS	
ADD TOTAL BONUS POINTS	◄
TOTAL SCORE	

BATTING TEAM NAME: _____ **Primary School**

BATS	BALLS BOWLED – SCORE PER								PROGRESSIVE	
Pair No:	1	2	3	4	5	6	RUNS	WICKET	RUNS	WICKETS
PAIR 1										
PAIR 2										
PAIR 3										
PAIR 4										

INNINGS – RUNS	
ADD TOTAL BONUS POINTS	◄
TOTAL SCORE	

TRANSFER BONUS POINTS

NB. Please complete section below

SCORES VERIFIED

TEAM 1: _____ **TEAM 2:** _____

MATCH WON BY: _____

Primary School – Kanga 8's Cricket
Rules of the Game

Figure 6.7 Kanga cricket scoresheet.

Vs. Frankston Primary School, who scored 75 runs and took 7 wickets

Frankston's score: 75 + (7 × 5) = 110

Frankston Primary School defeated Bentleigh Primary School.

Scoring in the Regional Carnivals and State Finals. The teams with the most wins after three games shall contest the Grand Final. In the event of more than two teams being on equal points, the team with the highest aggregate score shall continue on. If a result still cannot be determined, the side that has bowled the least number of 'no balls' shall be declared the winner.

SUPER 8s

Equipment. Incrediballs and wooden bats; pads and gloves for each player. It is also recommended that children wear boxes and helmets with a grill.

Number of players. Two teams of 8–10 players each (players can be interchanged between and during games—for example, player 9 bowls but does not bat, and player 8 bats only).

This is a variation of the Super 8s game that is played at a national level throughout the world. All games are played in accordance with the laws of cricket as recognised by the Australian Cricket Board and as adopted by the State and Territory cricket associations, except as amended in the following section.

Each innings consists of 8 × 6 ball overs, bowled by members of each side from one end of the wicket. All runs and extras are scored according to the accepted laws of cricket with the following exceptions:

- Any 'wide' or 'no ball' shall count as two extras to the batting side, and an extra ball shall be bowled at which the batter has a free hit, that is, the batter cannot be out bowled, caught, stumped, hit wicket, or leg before wicket (LBW). There will be a maximum of six deliveries in one over in the event of 'wides', 'no balls', or both.

- A ball called 'wide' by the umpire will be considered a dead ball. Two runs only will be scored, and batters cannot be out bowled, caught, stumped, hit wicket, or LBW from the next delivery; that is, the batter receives a free hit.

- Two lines shall be marked (or markers shall be placed) at right angles to the crease from the batting to the bowling crease, 80 cm from the line of the middle stumps, to assist the umpire (see figure 6.8). Any ball that passes outside the indicators (or hits them) shall be called a wide unless it strikes the bat or any part of the batter below the shoulders.
- A line or marker shall also be placed 5 m in front of the batting crease. Any delivery that pitches before this point shall be called 'no ball' (see figure 6.8).
- When the ball is delivered, no players may field closer than 10 m from the bat, except behind point where gully and orthodox slips will be permitted (see figure 6.9).

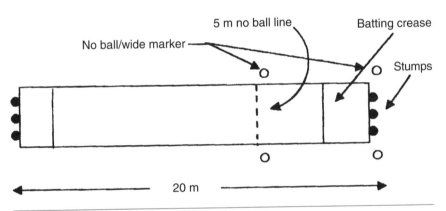

Figure 6.8 Batting crease.

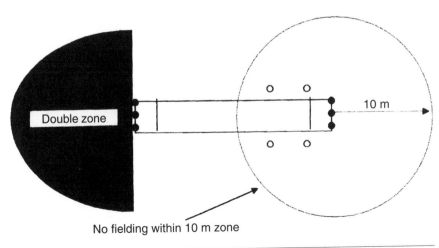

Figure 6.9 No fielding zone.

Bowlers bowl one over each per innings (depending on the time frame, there may be time for two overs per bowler and four overs for each batting pair). One bowler (or an additional player) may bowl the keeper's over if the keeper relinquishes his or her turn to bowl. Bowlers may bowl overarm or underarm. However, if underarm is chosen, the ball must bounce only once before reaching the batter, or it must reach the batter on the full below knee height. The delivery, if in breach of the preceding, shall be deemed a 'no ball'.

Players bat in pairs; number each pair from 1 to 4. Each pair bat for a total of two overs. Any runs scored in the Double Zone are multiplied by 2, for example, 2 = 4, 4 = 8, 6 = 12, and so on. Calculate the score by determining the number of runs made and multiplying it by the number of wickets taken. See scoresheet in figure 6.11.

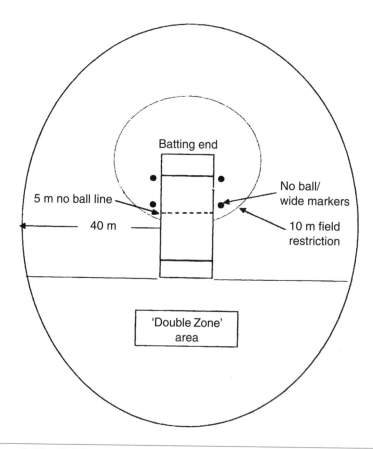

Figure 6.10   Cricket boundaries.

SUPER 8s
SCORESHEET

_____ VS _____

♦ MARK WICKET TAKEN WITH AN X
♦ MARK 'WIDES' AND 'NO BALLS' WITH A CIRCLE EG. ② OR ⑤
♦ 'WIDES' = 2 RUNS ONLY, 'NO BALLS' = 2 RUNS PLUS ANY SCORED

INNINGS OF: _____

BOWLERS NAME	BALLS BOWLED - SCORE/WICKET							TOTAL PER OVER	
	1	2	3	4	5	6		WICKETS	RUNS
1.									
2.									
3.									
4.									
5.									
6.									
7.									
8.									
					INNINGS - TOTAL				
					TEAM AVERAGE				

INNINGS OF: _____

BOWLERS NAME	BALLS BOWLED - SCORE/WICKET							TOTAL PER OVER	
	1	2	3	4	5	6		WICKETS	RUNS
1.									
2.									
3.									
4.									
5.									
6.									
7.									
8.									
					INNINGS - TOTAL				
					TEAM AVERAGE				

SCORES VERIFIED

UMPIRE: _____

Figure 6.11 Super 8s scoresheet.

FOUR QUARTERS CRICKET
(SUITABLE FOR AGES 12 AND UNDER)

Number of players.   8–12 per side

Equipment.   2 bats, 1 ball, 2 sets of stumps, and protective equipment if a hard ball is used

Suggested time frame.   4 half-hour sessions = 2 hours

Each game is divided into four half-hour quarters, with team A batting in the first and third quarters and team B batting in the second and fourth quarters. After 30 minutes, the batting team (team A) bowl the same amount of overs that they received in the first quarter. When team A bat again in the third quarter, the players who were batting at the end of the first quarter resume batting. Those players who did not bat in the first quarter each have a turn until the entire team has been dismissed.

If the entire team is dismissed within their allocated batting time, the batting lineup reverts back to the start, or alternatively players who were dismissed cheaply can return.

The aim of this format is as follows:

- To ensure that all players have a turn at batting, bowling, or both during each day's play

- To ensure that members of the batting team do not have to sit for long periods

Rules.   All runs and extras are scored according to the accepted laws of cricket with the following exceptions:

- Batters may be given out any of the traditional forms of dismissal. LBW shall not apply unless the batter does not play at the ball and deliberately protects his or her wicket with the body. Batters can go out first ball, and 'when you're out, you're out!'

- Any 'no balls' or 'wides' shall give the batter a free hit from the batting tee. The ball must be hit forward of square (i.e., a player cannot hit backward).

- Only six balls are bowled in one over. No extra deliveries will be bowled for 'wides' and 'no balls'.

- Markers placed behind the bowling end indicate the bonus area. (This is to encourage the players to straight drive when possible, especially on free hits.) Any runs scored in this area are doubled in value, for example, 3 runs = 6, 4 = 8, and so on, except that a straight run over the boundary is accredited as 10 runs.

Variations

- Players retire at 15, 20, or 25 runs.
- Bowlers rotate until each has bowled two overs (restrict length of run-ups).
- Playing areas are restricted (e.g., 40 m boundaries).
- The game is played with the Dual Pitch format.
- The game is played with the Super 8s format.
- Games are played over two days—four quarters each day (ensuring full rotations of batting and bowling).
- A player receives a free hit after a 'no ball' or 'wide'. A player cannot go out on a free hit except a run out.
- If tee hits are not employed, then no over continues after eight deliveries.
- If the eighth delivery is a 'no ball', then the first ball of the next over is a free hit.

Equipment

You're probably familiar with most standard pieces of cricket equipment: stumps, balls, bats, batting gloves, keeping gloves, pads, helmets, protectors, and so on. It's very important that these be in good repair and satisfy certain requirements.

Stumps and Bails

Stumps and bails act as the target for the bowlers and fielders to aim and are arguably the most significant pieces of equipment in the game of cricket—the game's trademark, if you like. Three stumps make up a set, and one set is placed at each end of the pitch. Traditionally, stumps are made from wood, but metal and plastic versions are also available and are often used for training and school cricket. Plastic stumps are more than adequate for younger cricketers, especially when the players are using soft varieties of balls.

Bails are pieces of wood that sit in the grooves on the top of the stumps. Each set of three stumps has two bails. You can introduce wooden stumps and bails when players begin to use leather balls.

Balls

The traditional cricket ball is made with layers of cork bound together with string and encased in a leather outer covering. A standard leather ball weighs 156 g, but a smaller, lighter version (142 g) is used for women's cricket games and has been adopted by some junior grades. Other balls are available for situations where leather versions are deemed unsuitable. Plastic versions such as the 'softaball' are acceptable for some youth competitions and for school cricket.

Kanga cricket balls are soft, plastic balls that bounce like real cricket balls yet are soft and light and therefore very safe. These are strongly favoured for use in junior (primary) school cricket and by young cricketers. Using these lighter, softer balls allows young players to develop their skills without being afraid of catching or batting the hard leather ball.

Bats

The traditional wooden bat has evolved over the years to the type we see today. The bat consists of two main parts. The blade, which forms the main part or body of the bat, provides the hitting surface. The handle, made mainly of cane, is inserted into the top of the blade. The blade of a senior bat is about 55 cm long and about 10–12 cm wide, with handles varying in length, shape, and thickness to suit individual preferences. Smaller versions are available for younger players.

Important factors to look for in a bat are as follows:

- Length—the top of the bat should reach to about the batter's hip.
- Weight—it is very important that younger players use lightweight bats. Many young players retard their development by using a favourite bat, handed down from their father or other relative, that is much too heavy.

For very young cricketers and the primary school cricket programme, the Kanga cricket bat is ideal. This is a very durable plastic version that has the feel of the real cricket bat. It is light, safe, and easy to swing.

Batting Gloves

As with most modern equipment, gloves today have changed dramatically, with improved design and new synthetic materials. They offer added protection for the fingers, thumbs, and back of the hands. Players should select properly fitting gloves that provide comfortable grip. Apart from protecting the hands, batting gloves also help prevent the bat from slipping in the hands.

Wicket-Keeping Gloves

The wicket keeper acts as the 'catcher' for the bowlers' bowling. Wicket-keeping gloves are heavily padded on the palms with rubber inserts for the fingers and thumbs, and the palm surface is covered with dimpled rubber. The rest of the glove consists mainly of leather, with a large leather webbing between the thumb and index finger. Young players should wear wicket-keeping gloves whenever possible, because wicket keepers need to become accustomed to catching and throwing the ball with them on. Again, players should select comfortable, properly fitting gloves. New gloves, which tend to be quite stiff, can be softened by placing them on a hard surface and hitting the palms with a wooden mallet or the toe of a cricket bat. Wearing cotton or chamois inner gloves (inners) can also provide added protection.

Pads (Leg Protectors)

Batting. Leg protectors or pads have made great advances in recent years with the development of sturdy, lightweight synthetic materials, such as nylon and polystyrene, that have replaced the heavier materials used in the past. In selecting batting pads, the younger cricketer should choose the type most suitable for the kind of ball being used and the level of competition. Pads must be the right size. If they are too small, they will not provide adequate protection; if they are too big, the player will not be able to move freely.

Wicket-Keeping. These are shorter versions of the batting pad and are designed to protect the keeper from the ankle to slightly above the knee.

Helmets

In terms of the history of the game, the helmet is a relatively new arrival. Made of strong, lightweight fibreglass, helmets provide protection to the skull and face. Strongly encourage your young players, especially when playing with a hard ball, to wear helmets both when batting and when wicket keeping. Helmets should also be fitted with an appropriate grill to protect the facial area. They should be of an appropriate size, and the grill should be tightly adjusted so that the gap between the top of the grill and the peak of the helmet is smaller than the ball.

Not only do helmets help protect the player, but they also give the players much more confidence—for example, for batters to play short-pitch bowling and wicket keepers to practise their craft against fast bowlers. It is highly recommended that a keeper who is not wearing a helmet or a grill at least wear a mouth guard.

Protectors

Protectors are available in a large range of sizes and are generally made of a very durable plastic. This should be the first piece of personal equipment that male players acquire when embarking on a competitive cricket career. Players should be encouraged to wear them not only when batting and keeping but also when fielding. The protector should be an appropriate size and worn under a snugly fitting undergarment so as to keep it firmly in position.

Batting Tees

The batting tee, a sort of inverted cone from which a ball can be hit, is a very useful piece of equipment for both minor games and training skills and drills. Used under normal conditions, they are virtually indestructible and will be a long-term investment. Batting tees can be purchased through the Australian Cricket Board.

Game Procedures

Following certain procedures at the start of the game ensures that the game runs smoothly and that coaches on both teams are aware of any special rules for the playing field or boundaries. Here are some elements common to cricket games:

- The home team sets up the stumps and the boundaries (if required).
- The home team tosses the coin for the visiting captain to call. The captain winning the toss determines whether his or her team will bat or bowl.
- Each team has 11 players participating in the game at any time (although coaches may agree to variances of this rule).

Other variations in procedure include the following:

- Teams can bat or bowl more than 11 players.
- Teams play 12 per side with a designated batter and bowler (i.e., one player can either bat only or bowl only).
- The team batting first generally can bat for a limited time or a limited number of overs; then when the other team has their turn to bat, they receive the same number of overs each.

Except in modified games, a batter can be out a number of ways, some of which include

- bowled—when the bowler bowls the ball and hits the stumps after being missed by the batter;
- caught out—a member of the fielding team catches a ball hit by the batter, before it touches the ground and whilst still in the field of play;
- hit wicket—when the batter hits or stands on the stumps in the process of hitting, trying to hit, or trying to avoid the bowled ball;
- stumped—when, in attempting to hit the ball, the batter moves out of his or her crease and misses the ball, and the wicket keeper dislodges the bails with the ball in hand;
- run out—when, on attempting to make a run, the wickets are broken by the fielders at the end the batter is running to before reaching the crease; and

- leg before wicket—when the ball hits a batter and the umpire considers that it was pitched in a straight line between the wickets, or on the off side, and would have hit the stumps.

Some less-common ways of being dismissed include when a player handles the ball, interference, and 'timed out'. Being timed out can occur if, at the fall of a wicket, the umpire feels that the incoming batter is deliberately wasting time so as to gain some advantage for his or her team. On appeal from the fielding team, the umpire can give the new batter out.

A batter scores a run by hitting the ball and running up and down the length of the pitch. Each time one length is run, one run is scored, so if a batter and his or her partner each complete three lengths of the pitch, then three runs are scored. If the ball passes over the boundary, then four runs are attributed to the batting team. If the ball passes over the boundary and lands on the other side, then the batting team is accredited with six runs.

If the batters complete laps of the pitch after the wicket keeper fails to stop the ball, which has not touched the bat or the batter's body, then byes are scored—one bye for each length of the pitch (or lap) the batters cover (or four runs if the ball crosses the boundary along the ground).

A 'wide' is signalled when the umpire considers the bowled ball so far away from the batter that he or she cannot play a legitimate cricket shot at the ball. The batting team is accredited with one run.

A 'no ball' should be called if the bowler fails to keep some part of his or her front foot behind the batting crease, or if the bowler delivers the ball whilst the back foot is outside the return crease.

Any delivery deemed to be a 'wide' or 'no ball' is bowled again. For more detailed information on rules and playing conditions, consult publications such as those available in libraries and state and territory controlling bodies.

Umpires

Umpires are officials who enforce the rules of the game. Junior games are usually umpired by the coach or manager from each team—one at the bowler's end and the other at square leg. Umpire signals are demonstrated in figure 6.12.

Figure 6.12 Umpire signals.

The umpire at the bowler's end decides whether the ball is a 'wide' or a 'no ball'. That umpire also decides when the batter has been caught out or LBW or run out at the nonstriker's (or bowler's) end. The umpire at square leg can call a 'no ball' above shoulder height (this rule varies from association to association), adjudicates on run outs and stumpings, and on rare occasions calls the bowler for throwing.

Like you, these umpires are generally volunteers, not professionals. Consequently, from time to time they will make mistakes. How you react when you think the umpire has erred is important. Be a good role model for your players. If you think a ruling is incorrect, quickly and calmly discuss it with the umpire, or accept it. Do not become involved in an argument, make gestures venting your disagreement, or mutter in front of your players about the decision.

Fielding Positions

Cricket is played with 11 players on the field in defence. The busiest of these are the bowlers and the wicket keeper. Fielders are placed in positions as depicted in figure 6.13, and those out near the boundary are referred to as outfielders.

Players close to the bat can be positioned in places known as silly mid off, silly mid on, silly point, and short leg. These are very attacking positions that are stationed as such to take catches that pop up from defensive batting strokes. Such positions are generally discouraged or disallowed in junior cricket.

One of your biggest coaching decisions involves deciding who should play which position. Here are some tips to help you choose wisely. Remember, however, that whenever possible, you should give all your players the opportunity to experience different positions.

- Put your strongest throwers in the outfield.
- Players who perform well at reflex catches should be favoured for positions such as slips and gully, and those who are quick and agile should be favoured in the cover and mid-wicket positions.
- Some players will naturally take to wicket keeping; however, very young aspiring wicket keepers should still attempt to develop other skills, such as the different forms of bowling.

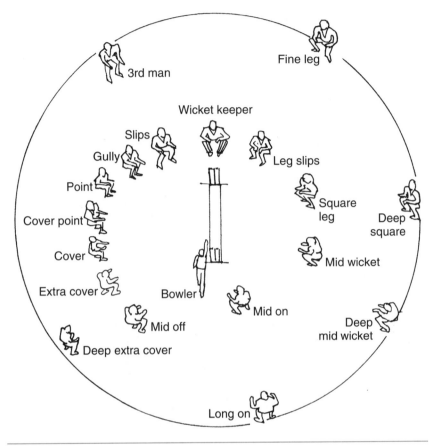

Figure 6.13 Fielding positions.

Keeping Score

The novice scorer may find the scorebook or scoresheet a daunting sight when initially recruited to the job. There are some complications due to idiosyncrasies of some rules, but in general, if the scorer follows the procedure suggested here, the task should not be as difficult as it may at first appear.

Fill in the details at the top, such as the competition, club, date, and so forth. Fill in the batting team's lineup under 'Batsmen' or 'Batters'. Write down at least the first two opening bowlers in the 'Bowlers' column.

Now the game is about to commence. Work to a pattern; for example, start at the bottom of the page and work up. Step 1: The bowler bowls the ball. If it is not scored off, then simply register by placing a dot in the appropriate place next to the bowler.

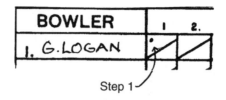

Step 1

The next ball is bowled, the batter hits the ball, and the batters run two runs. Step 2: The scorer registers the score in this manner.

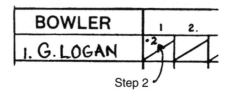

Step 2

Step 3: Then go to the running total and mark off two runs.

Step 3

```
      1 2 3 4 5 6 7 8 9
10
20
30
40
50
60
70
80
90
```

Step 4: Then move up the page to the batter's name and accredit the striker with the two runs.

Step 4

BATTER	RUNS AS SCORED	HOW OUT	BOWLER	TOTALS
1. BEN SMITH 2				
2. KIM JONES				

When the bowler takes a wicket, it is registered in the 'Bowling' section and denoted with an X or a W.

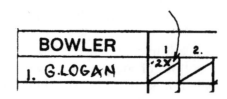

Step 5: Now move up the sheet to the next relevant section, 'Fall of Wicket'.

	1	2	3	4	5	6	7	8	9	100	1	2	3	4	5	6	7	8	9	200	1	2
10										110										210		
20										120										220		
30										130										230		
40										140										240		
50										150										250		
60										160										260		
70										170										270		
80										180										280		
90										190										290		

SCORE AT FALL OF EACH WICKET	1. 2		2.
BATTER OUT	B. SMITH		
NOT OUT BATTER	K. JONES (0)		

Step 2

RESULT	WON/LOST	1st INNINGS OUTRIGHT

BOWLER	1	2.	3	4	5
Step 1 → 1. G. LOGAN	•2x				

Step 6: Then move up to the 'Batting' section. The batter who has just gone out has the symbol >> marked at the end of his or her running total.

Step 7: Then, moving across to the right of the page, fill in the 'How Out' section, and include the successful bowler's name in the box provided.

The 'Batting' section will then appear as follows:

BATTER		RUNS AS SCORED	HOW OUT	BOWLER	TOTALS
1. BEN SMITH	2 >>		BOWLED	G. LOGAN	2
2. KIM JONES					
3.					
4.					
5.					
6.					
7.					
8.					
9.					
10.					
11.					

Should the batter be dismissed by being caught (e.g., batter no. 2), then the player taking the catch is registered on the sheet; or if the batter is run out (e.g., batter no. 3), then that would be denoted as such (see below).

BATTER	RUNS AS SCORED	HOW OUT	BOWLER	TOTALS
1. BEN SMITH	2	BOWLED	G. LOGAN	2
2. KIM JONES	12 11141432 11111212C	CAUGHT M. LIDDELL	B. HEPPELL	36
3. JOE HEAZELWOOD	11			

The full scoresheet will now appear like this:

'No balls' and 'wides' are usually indicated by a dot with a circle, N, or W.

These are then recorded in the extras or 'Sundries' section along with byes and leg byes:

BYES			TOTAL SUNDRIES	
LEG BYES	I		**TOTAL SCORE**	
WIDES				
NO-BALLS	I			

Any over completed without runs being scored from the bat and without any 'wides' or 'no balls' being bowled is termed a maiden over and is denoted as follows:

Other extras such as byes and leg byes are entered into the 'Sundries' section but are *not* included in the bowler's running tally.

Cricket has standard abbreviation symbols that are useful to know when keeping a scorebook:

B	Bye	ST	Stumped
LB	Leg bye	M	Maiden
LBW	Leg before wicket	W	Wide
CHT	Caught	NB	No ball
BLO	Bowled	DEC	Declared
RO	Run out	CC	Compulsory closure

Cricket Terms

Cricket has its own vocabulary. Becoming familiar with common cricket terms will make your job easier.

12th man—The 12th member of the team who can take an injured team member's position on the field. This player can only field; he or she may not bowl or bat.

appeal—A shout or statement made to the umpire for the batter to be given out. An appeal by the fielding side must be made for a batter to be given out. 'How's that?' is a popular appeal by cricketers.

declaration—When the captain of the batting side ends an innings (usually first innings) before all 10 team members are out.

draw—An unfinished match. Neither team has been beaten; one or both of the teams have not finished two innings; the side batting last has not scored sufficient runs to pass the opposition's score, nor have they lost 10 wickets.

follow on—When the batting side bats immediately again after finishing their first innings, due to their not getting within a set number of runs of their opposition's first innings score.

runner—Any team member of the batting side who runs between wickets for an injured batter.

Batting Terms

backward defence—When the batter moves back across his or her wicket to hit a short-pitched ball down into the ground, once again without a follow-through and with top hand dominance.

cut—A shot played at a short-pitched ball outside the off stump. The batter moves back across his or her wicket and cuts down on the ball, causing it to be hit into the ground onto the off side and behind the wicket, for example, square cut or late cut, as shown in figure 6.14.

drive—An attacking shot played by the batter in the hope of scoring runs. The batter moves forward into the ball, facing the direction in which he or she wants the ball to go, hits the ball with the full face of the bat, and follows through. Depending on the pitch of the ball, the batter can hit different position drives, such as off, on, cover, or straight, as shown in figure 6.14.

forward defence—When a batter hits the ball in a defensive manner, not trying to score runs but purely to stop it from hitting the stumps. The batter moves forward on his or her front foot and hits the ball down into the ground without any follow-through and with dominance of the top hand.

hook—A horizontal bat shot played by the batter when the ball is short and going down the leg side. The batter moves inside the line of the ball and pivots around, hitting the ball toward fine leg.

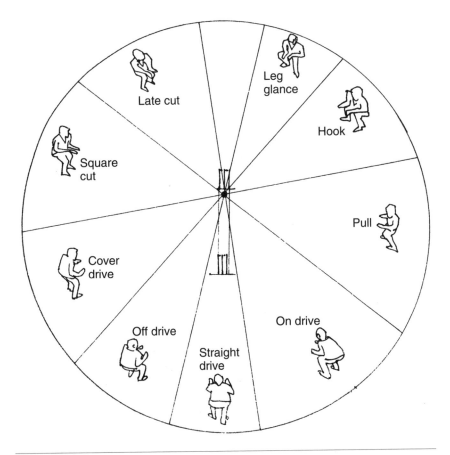

Figure 6.14 Batting positions.

leg glance—A shot played by the batter when the ball is in line with the stumps or on leg side. The batter moves inside the path of the ball and deflects the ball off his or her pads, down leg side behind the wicket.

pull shot—A shot played by the batter when a short-pitched ball is in line with the body. The batter moves across inside the path of the ball, hitting the ball with a horizontal bat down into the ground by turning the wrist over. The pull shot is played on the leg side.

sweep—A horizontal bat shot played by the batter when the ball is pitched up outside leg stump. The batter goes down on his or her back knee to place the ball on the leg side, to square leg, or behind the wicket.

Fielding Position Terms

allrounder—A player who is equally competent in batting, bowling, and fielding skills.

cover—A fielding position. Usually at a 45-degree angle to the batter at stance on the off side, halfway to the boundary.

cover point—A fielding position. Similar to cover but square to the wicket on the off side.

deep square leg—A fielding position on the on side, square of the wicket, on the boundary.

extra cover—A fielding position on the off side, placed between mid-off and cover.

fielding—The part of the game involving catching, stopping, chasing, and throwing the ball.

fine leg—A fielding position on the on side, behind the wicket, near the boundary.

gully—A fielding position on the off side; a close catching position between slips and cover point.

leg side field—Those positions set on the side of the batter at stance.

leg slip—A close catching position just behind the wicket on the on side.

mid off—A position on the off side usually behind the bowler's crease and just slightly to the bowler's left.

mid on—Same as mid-off, but on the on side.

mid wicket—An on-side fielding position. About a 45-degree angle from the batter at his stance.

misfield—A term used to denote the missing of a ball hit toward the fielder.

off side—The side of the field in front of the batter taking up a side-on stance.

on side—The side of the field behind the batter's back taking up a side-on stance.

outfield—That part of the ground that forms the extremities. Long throws and high catches are from these parts of the ground.

overthrows—Additional runs scored by the batter as a result of the fielding side misfielding the ball thrown toward the wicket keeper or bowler.

return—When the fielder throws the ball in to the wicket keeper or a player positioned close to the stumps.

short backward square leg—A fielding position on the on side, in a close catching position just behind the batting crease.

silly mid off—A close catching position on the off side in front of the wicket.

silly mid on—A close catching position on the on side in front of the wicket.

slips—Fielding positions behind the wicket on the off side; catching positions waiting to intercept edged shots.

slips cordon—A series of slip fielders in a pattern as set by the fielding captain.

spill a catch—To drop a catch.

square leg—A fielding position on the on side, square of the batting crease.

stumped—A batter is out stumped if, having played at the ball, he is out of his ground when the wicket keeper breaks the wicket.

the take (wicket keeping)—Catching the ball.

thirdman—A position near the boundary behind the wicket on the off side.

throwing in—Returning the ball to the wicket keeper or a player positioned near the stumps at the bowler's end.

wicket keeper—Fielding position behind the wicket to receive the ball if it is not hit. The wicket keeper wears gloves and pads.

Bowling Terms

approach—A bowler's run-up to the wicket before the delivery stride.

delivery—The bowling of the ball.

fasties—Slang term that refers to the team's quick bowlers (also referred to as fast bowlers).

fast wicket—A wicket that is usually hard and well grassed. The ball bounces and skids very quickly onto the batter.

flipper—A variation of a leg spinner's bowling repertoire. The ball is held between the thumb and index finger. It skids straight through and comes off the wicket very quickly.

good length—That spot on the wicket where a bowler tries to land the ball so that the batter cannot get onto the front foot to drive or push back onto the back foot to cut or pull.

googly—A leg spinner's variation bowled with a leg break action that comes out of the back of the hand. Instead of spinning away from the batsman, it spins back toward him or her. Also called *wrong'un*.

hat trick—When a bowler takes three wickets (dismissing three batters) with consecutive balls, not necessarily in the same over.

inswinger—A fast-medium bowler's variation; a ball that swings in the air from the off side toward the leg side.

leg before wicket (LBW)—A method of dismissal. Generally a batter is out LBW if the ball hits a batter and the umpire considers that it was pitched on a straight line between the wickets or on the off side and would have hit the wicket.

leg break—A slow bowler's variation; a ball that spins away from a right-handed batter after hitting the pitch.

leg cutters—A medium pacer's variation; a ball that hits the pitch on the seam of the ball and cuts away from the right-handed batter.

leg spin—See *leg break*.

line and length—The term given to bowling with accuracy; bowling straight and not too short or too full.

loose ball—A ball that has been delivered very erratically and presents the batter with an easy scoring chance.

maiden over—An over that has been bowled without a run being scored off it.

no ball—For a delivery to be fair, the ball must be bowled, not thrown. If either umpire is not entirely satisfied with the absolute fairness of a delivery in this respect he or she shall call and signal 'no ball' instantly upon delivery. The umpire at the bowler's wicket shall call and signal 'no ball' if, in the delivery stride, no part of the bowler's front foot is behind the popping crease, or if the umpire is not satisfied that the bowler's back foot has landed within and not touching the return crease or its forward extension (see figure 6.15). As the ball is an illegal delivery, the bowler is given an extra delivery in that over.

off break—A spin bowler's variation; a ball that spins from the off side toward the leg side.

off cutter—A pace bowler's variation; the ball cuts off the seam from the off side toward the leg side or into the right-handed batter.

off spin—See *off break*.

outswinger—A fast bowler's variation; a ball that swings through the air from the on side toward the off side.

Fair delivery

No ball
The bowler's back foot touches
or lands on or outside the return
crease.

Fair delivery

No ball
The bowler in the delivery stride
has no part of the front foot
behind the popping crease.

Figure 6.15   No ball.

over—Consists normally of six balls bowled by a bowler from either
end of the wicket before changing to the other end, where another bowler will commence the first of the next six balls.

pace—The speed of the ball as it flies through the air or bounces off
the pitch toward the batter.

pitch—The surface on which the game is played; specifically, the
batting and bowling sections of the ground.

popping crease—The line 1.2 m in front of the wicket on or behind
which the batter must ground the bat to avoid being stumped or
run out and on or behind which the bowler must ground his or
her front foot to avoid being 'no balled'.

return crease—A line running at right angles from the popping crease, inside of which the bowler must ground the back foot at the moment of delivery.

run-up—A bowler's approach to the wicket before and during delivery.

seamer—A bowler who depends on using the seam of the ball to cut the ball off the pitch.

short-pitched delivery—A ball that is delivered so that it will rise up off the pitch; forces the batter to go onto the back foot.

slow wicket—A wicket where the ball comes off its surface in a very slow manner.

spinner—A slow bowler who uses the fingers or wrist to cause the ball to deviate off the pitch when it bounces.

sticky wicket—A wicket that is affected by overnight rain and is beginning to dry out in the sun. This condition causes the ball to do unpredictable things and makes batting extremely hard.

stock bowler—A bowler who bowls long spells of accurate run-containing overs, often without a great deal of return with regard to wicket-taking success.

top spinner—A leg-spinner's variation; instead of spinning away toward the off side of a right-handed batter, the ball just spins through straight without deviation.

wicket—A combination of three stumps and two bails makes up a wicket.

wide ball—A ball bowled too high or too wide of the stumps for the batter to reach from the normal batting position.

wrist spinner—A term given to a bowler who bowls top spinners or googlies.

wrong'un—See *googly*.

Unit 7

What Cricket Skills and Drills Should I Teach?

In unit 4, you learned how to teach cricket skills and how to plan practices. Now it's time to consider exactly what cricket skills to emphasise and which drills will help your players develop those skills. Cricket involves many skills, and you can't teach them all at once. The best way is to look at them as separate categories. These categories are batting, bowling, wicket keeping, and fielding.

Batting

Although it's generally necessary that players adhere to certain fundamentals in batting, always remember that every player has his or her own individual style. When coaching youth cricket, a coach's objective should be to develop a safe and effective method of batting.

The key points of batting are as follows:

- Concentration—the player must maintain a fine focus on every ball from the bowler's hand on to the face of the bat.

- Technique—the player must align body levers, keep hands in close to the body, and allow the front elbow to push through in the direction of the shots.

- Balance—the player must hit off a stable base by adjusting body weight to the length of the ball and positioning the head in line with the ball.

Concentration

The batter should be in a state of awareness between deliveries but must raise this level to one of extreme concentration as the bowler is about to deliver the ball. Former Australian captain and coach Bob Simpson refers to this as the 'Now' technique (see figure 7.1).

Players can use visual cues, such as observing how the ball increases in size or noting the angle of the seam during flight. They may try to identify the direction the ball will swing, or perhaps which side is the shiny one.

Figure 7.1 The 'Now' technique.

Concentration Drills

Name. Seam Observation

Organisation. A batter in stance position with gloves on stands 5 m from his or her partner. The partner underarms the ball for the batter to catch, with the seam in straight-on, cross, inswinger, or outswinger position (see figure 7.2). The batter calls out the seam position during flight, then calls out the position the ball is in when it is at rest in his or her gloves.

Variations

- The partner alters the spin of the ball; the batter calls 'leg spin', 'off spin', or 'top spin'.
- Batting in the nets, facing bowlers using balls with distinctive seams or bicoloured balls (or normal balls), the batter calls the type of delivery as the ball is released. The coach monitors the responses from behind and issues questions such as, 'Why did you think that delivery would be an inswinger?'

Figure 7.2 Seam observation drill.

Name. Tracking

Organisation. A batter with gloves on stands 5 m from his or her partner. The partner underarms a marked bean bag from behind the back to the batter, who catches it with head over bag (see figure 7.3). The batter calls out the marking on the bean bag (X, number, O, or colour) during flight, then checks the bag after it is in the gloves.

Variation. Use different types of balls (plastic, composition, leather, tennis).

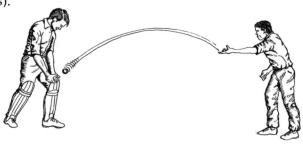

Figure 7.3 Tracking drill.

Name.   Chin-Downs

Organisation.   One partner underarms the ball to a batter 5 m away. The batter maintains his or her body position on contact with the bat. Either the partner or the coach monitors the batter's chin and head positions (see figure 7.4).

Variations

- The partner full-volleys short and varied throws.
- The partners progress through overarm throws to bowling.

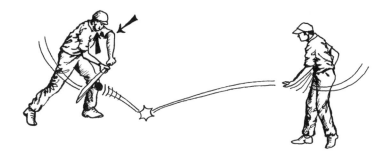

Figure 7.4   Chin-downs drill.

Name.   Ball Bounce

Organisation.   One partner throws the ball to the batter, who plays the appropriate shot (see figure 7.5). The batter then estimates where the ball bounced on the pitch and moves a marker to that spot. The partners then compare the marker position with the partner's observations. The partners progress to bowled balls.

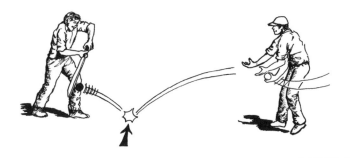

Figure 7.5   Ball bounce drill.

Name. Hand and Arm Motion

Organisation. The coach or a proficient partner releases the ball with different spinning motions (see figure 7.6). The batter describes the hand motion and links it in with ball movement. Vary with inswinger, outswinger, off cutter, and leg cutter arm and hand motions. The batter calls out the type of delivery and then

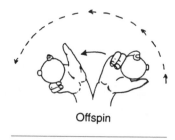

Offspin

Figure 7.6 Hand and arm motion drill.

discusses with the partner or coach the type of action used and how that caused the subsequent movement of the ball through the air or off the pitch.

Technique

The ability to make effective shots is greatly enhanced by a good setup of grip, stance, and backlift. Teach your young players proper technique right from the start.

Grip

As a coach, you should be aware that all batters grip the bat in slightly different ways. Be prepared to allow for individual differences.

For the basic recommended grip, lay the bat facedown on the ground with the handle pointing toward the batter. The batter then picks the bat up with both hands together in the middle of the handle (see figure 7.7)

Figure 7.7 Correct hand position for the basic bat grip.

The V formed by the first finger and the thumb should be pointing down the bat between the splice and the leading edge (see figures 7.8 and 7.9).

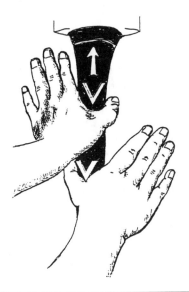

Figure 7.8   The first finger and thumb form a V.

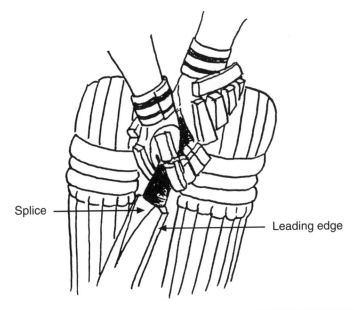

Figure 7.9   The V formed by the hands points down the bat.

Stance

Teach your young cricketers to adopt a comfortable stance, with feet approximately shoulder-width apart, knees slightly flexed, and weight evenly balanced, as in figure 7.10. The eyes should be level. Emphasise the value of keeping the eyes level with the following drill.

Figure 7.10 Correct batting stance.

Have your players stand facing a brick or very solid wall and underarm the ball against the wall so they can make continuous catches. Have them perform this first with the head tilted to the side, then with the eyes level. It will become obvious to them that their eyes see the ball much more effectively when level.

In the stance, the chin should be above the toes from front on and midway between the feet from side on; this helps keep the centre of gravity over the base of support. If the head is over too far, (i.e., toward the off side), then the batter tends to fall to the off side, greatly limiting his or her ability to play on the leg side.

Flexed knees will enable quick, balanced movements both forward and backward. An imaginary line drawn between both sets of toes should point directly toward the bowler. Similarly, an imaginary line drawn from hip joint to hip joint will point in the same direction, thus bringing the body into a side-on position. Adding a slightly open shoulder position provides a more comfortable stance.

Rest the bottom of the bat against the little toe of the back foot (this may vary; e.g., some batters prefer to place the bat in front of the back foot). Finally, the knuckles of the top hand should rest against the front thigh.

Here are some key points to emphasise with regard to stance:

- Stand with feet shoulder-width apart.
- Stand side on.
- Keep the knees relaxed and slightly bent.
- Keep the eyes level.
- Weight should be on the balls of the feet.

Taking Guard

Next, the batter attempts to establish exactly where he or she is standing in relation to the line of the middle stumps, which is taking guard (see figure 7.11). The most common request is centre, or the middle stump. The batter then makes a mark on the pitch as to where centre is.

Figure 7.11 Taking guard means lining up with the middle stump.

Backlift

The preparatory backlift, or backswing, occurs when the batter lifts the bat as the bowler is about to deliver the ball. The bat should be picked up in the direction of somewhere between first slip and middle stump. A backlift that goes any wider than that—for example, toward point or toward fine leg—will restrict the number of shots that a batter can play.

Some key points to emphasise with the backlift are as follows:

- Keep the head still.
- Coordinate the backlift with the bowler's delivery stride.

- Keep the hands in close to the body.
- The toe of the bat should point between off stump and second slip.

The proper backlift allows for a correct and efficient down-swing and for free stroke play on either side of the wicket. The coach should use the key points as a checklist. The bat should pivot from the front thigh so the hands do not move away from the line of the body during the backlift. This will also help the batter to maintain balance and also to keep the head in line with the ball. The wrist will cock naturally as the bat is swung back, opening the face slightly. The arms and bat will form a figure 9, or a number 6 in the backlift (see figure 7.12).

Figure 7.12   In the backlift position, the arms form a number 6.

Backlift Drills

Name.   **Height and Line**

Organisation.   One partner stands behind and facing the batter with palms down at bail height in a line between off stump and second slip. The batter practises backlift to just touch the partner's hands (see figure 7.13). The players exchange roles after 10 practices.

Variations

- Use video to analyse net/match backlift height and line.
- Perform the drill using only one hand.

Once players have developed the basic pattern, it is more productive for them to consider the effectiveness of the backlift as an integral part of the various strokes. Remember, the backlift is actually part of the stroke and not a skill in itself.

Figure 7.13   Height and line drill.

Name.   Timing

Organisation.   The batter and the bowler practise in a net situation. The coach calls 'up' as the bowler gathers to deliver. The batter responds, lifting the bat on the coach's call.

Variations

- The batter, rather than the coach, calls 'up' or 'now'.
- During a normal net session, an observer records the position of the bat at set times (e.g., as the bowler delivers or leaps) and reports to the batter or the coach during or after the practice session.
- Use video to analyse backlift timing (net/match).

Error Detection and Correction for the Backlift

Error

1. Player is late in initiating the backlift.

2. Player controls the bat with the bottom hand.

3. The backlift is directed toward the point area.

4. The backlift is looped in a circular motion.

5. The batter takes arms away from the body.

Correction

1. Repeat the Timing drill.

2. Practise lifting the bat with the top hand only.

3. Use stumps or plastic tubing to mark a channel for the backlift direction.

4. Stand the batter close to a wall and practise the backlift.

Set-Up Drill

Name.   Set-Up Drill

Organisation.   The grip, stance, and guard are best treated together in that they form the preparatory position for all stroke play. The batter takes up his or her stance at crease, and a partner then takes the steps illustrated in figure 7.14.

Review the following key points for the backlift:

- Cock the wrist at the top of the backlift.
- Lift toward the off stump.
- The arms and bat form a figure 9.
- Keep hands in close to the body.
- Keep the head still.

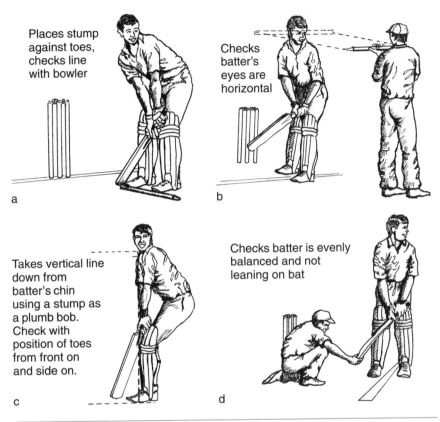

Places stump against toes, checks line with bowler

a

Checks batter's eyes are horizontal

b

Takes vertical line down from batter's chin using a stump as a plumb bob. Check with position of toes from front on and side on.

c

Checks batter is evenly balanced and not leaning on bat

d

Figure 7.14   Set-up drill: the partner performs the checks shown in *a*, *b*, *c*, and *d*.

Balance

Balance is vital for efficient stroke making. Most young people are well balanced while engaging in the everyday motor skills of running, jumping, skipping, and so on, but some become awkward and uncoordinated when swinging the cricket bat.

For young cricketers to hit the ball consistently with good timing and power and in the intended direction, they must be well balanced, with the feet stable and the centre of gravity over the base of support.

The head needs to be in line with the ball. Should the head move outside the line of the feet, the batter will lose control, power, and bat speed. The three most common fundamental errors that hinder balance (and safety) in young batters are in the table that follows.

Error Detection and Correction for Balance

Error

1. Some batters commit themselves only down an offside line irrespective of where the ball pitches. When the ball pitches on leg side, the batter will therefore have to play around the front leg to try to hit the ball.

2. Likewise, a little step with the front foot across the crease may result in the centre of gravity falling forward and outside the base of support. This will result in the player falling forward and also stepping forward with the back foot in an attempt to gain balance.

3. Young players who are afraid of being hit, especially those who play with a hard ball and no leg protection, tend to develop the bad habit of stepping away to the leg side (usually with the back foot) before or at delivery.

Correction

1. Roll the ball to different lines (i.e., outside off stump, on the stumps, toward the leg stump) and have the player drive the ball to different parts of the field.

2. Constant drill work will ingrain the 'head-to-line' movement.

3. Constant drill work, starting with soft balls (e.g., tennis balls) will help establish confidence. If the problem is that the player is moving the back foot toward square leg, it will help if the coach gets the player to move that foot (the right foot for right-handers) back and toward the off side.

Batting to Spin. The junior cricket coach needs to develop confidence and technique in junior players, to leave the crease to create half-volleys or to defend the flighted ball from spin bowlers. Leaving the crease is not a commitment to play attacking shots but merely an intention. Each young player needs to follow the balance drill variations aimed at combating the spinner, developing their own method such as shuffling down the pitch or using the crossover steps to the spinner (see figure 7.15).

Figure 7.15 Use crossover steps to the spinner.

Balance Drills

Name. Stationary Ball

Organisation. Three balls are placed on the pitch, one forward on off side, one forward on leg side, and one back on off side (see figure 7.16). The batter steps to the ball nominated by the coach. The coach checks that the batter's head is over the ball and the foot alongside. Progress to rehearsed defensive shots with the ball on a tee (use a low tee for forward and a high tee or open Kanga stump for back).

Figure 7.16 Stationary ball drill.

Name. Thrown Ball

Organisation. A partner or the coach lobs the ball to a batter in stance position. The batter catches it on the full, beside the front knee. The player maintains position so the coach can check the position of the head and feet as well as balance. Progress from off side across to on side, varying the side; to taking the ball on a half-volley; and to defensive shots with the bat, on full and then varied length. Repeat these progressions with the batter moving down the pitch to spinners (ball lobbed above the batter's eye level).

Name. Rolled Ball

Organisation. The batter is positioned in stance. A partner or the coach rolls the ball along off the stump line, and the batter stops it with the foot (side on or under the toe with the heel on the ground). See figure 7.17. Progress from off side across to on side, then vary the side. Progress to defensive stop with the bat. Have the batter stay in position after stopping so the coach can check the position of the head and feet as well as balance.

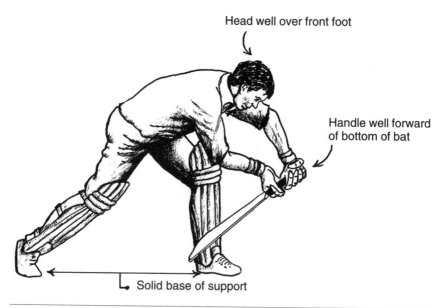

Figure 7.17 Rolled ball drill.

Name. Foot Angles

Organisation. The ball is placed on a tee for the batter to drive it toward a marked target. A pair of loose stumps are on the ground; the batter places the foot between them to develop the correct foot angle (see figure 7.18). Change the position of the tee, the targets, and the stump angles for a full range of drives.

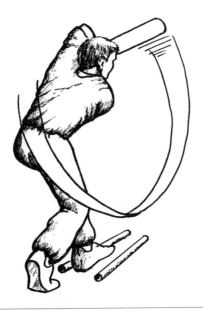

Figure 7.18 Foot angles drill.

Name. Judging Line (Advanced)

Organisation. Mark the bowling line along the middle stump. The ball is thrown on a half-volley; the batter scores a point for hitting the ball to the appropriate side of the wicket (see figure 7.19).

Variations

- Pitch balls shorter (back foot shots).
- Include markers for the batter to score bonus points: for pull shots or if two markers placed behind a square leg or in front of square apart, any ball hit between the markers scores a bonus of five points.

Figure 7.19 Judging line drill.

- Include hoops or circles drawn on the ground for the thrower to score points. Every time the thrower lands the ball in the specified circle, he earns five bonus points (the players add their batting points to their throwing points).

Judging Length

The following drills should help your players improve their judgment of length—that is, where the ball will pitch or land after the bowler releases it. Early assessment of length will help a player decide whether to move forward to the ball or move back.

Key points for judging length include the following:

- Fine focus on the hand projecting the ball.

- Track the ball.
- Initiate the appropriate movement, forward or back.

Judging Length Drill

Name.   Length Drill

Organisation.   Mark the bowling line at an appropriate length in front of the batter. Draw the batting lines a step in front of and behind the batter. The ball is thrown randomly to land before or after the bowling line. The batter plays with one foot past the appropriate line to score a point (the back foot is behind the back line for a short ball; the front foot is over the front line for a pitched-up ball). See figure 7.20.

Variations

- Include markers for the batter to score bonus points.
- Include hoops (or draw circles on the pitch in chalk) for the thrower to score points.

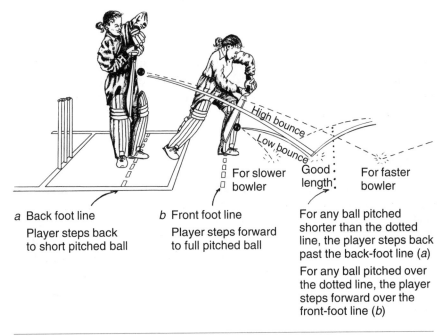

High bounce

Low bounce

For slower bowler

Good length

For faster bowler

a Back foot line

Player steps back to short pitched ball

b Front foot line

Player steps forward to full pitched ball

For any ball pitched shorter than the dotted line, the player steps back past the back-foot line (*a*)

For any ball pitched over the dotted line, the player steps forward over the front-foot line (*b*)

Figure 7.20   Length drill.

Error Detection and Correction for Judging Length

Error

1. The batter fails to focus on the release point.

2. The batter fails to track the ball (takes eyes off the ball).

3. The batter's body movement alters the focal length or direction.

4. The batter is not fully concentrating on the bowler.

Correction

1. Throw balls with different markings to help the player focus.

2. Use a field cradle (or roller) to make balls come at odd angles and heights.

3. Use a soft ball (e.g., tennis ball) and throw the ball at the batter in his or her normal stance. The batter ducks, sways, or evades the ball to remain in the crease area.

Front Foot Shots

Front foot shots are cricket shots, generally with vertical swing of the bat and hitting in the intended direction forward of the batter. They are played to deliveries that band on the half-volley close to the batter, low but on the full.

Front Foot Defence

When the batter is playing forward, the front shoulder leans into the ball (see figure 7.21) with the front knee bent to keep the body and head down. The back leg straightens, with only the toe remaining on the ground (unless the batter is moving down the pitch to a spinner). The batter should feel balanced in this position and takes only a 'natural' step forward—that is, he or she avoids overextending.

Key points to emphasise with the front foot defence include the following:

- Watch the ball.
- Keep the head still.
- Step toward the line of the ball.
- Transfer weight onto the front foot.
- Soft hands. Don't grip the bat too tightly as this will cause the ball to rebound further down the bat (thus more likely to be caught).
- Full face of the bat. In other words, don't

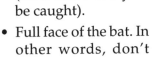

Figure 7.21 The correct position for the front foot defence.

have the bat on an angle. Full face of the bat will provide the maximum surface area with which to meet the ball.

Front Foot Leg Glance

This is merely an extension of the front foot defensive shot. The shot is played in line with the front leg, and just as impact is about to be made, the bat is turned slightly, causing the ball to run off into the fine leg area (see figure 7.22).

Figure 7.22 Turn the bat slightly just before the ball hits it.

Error Detection and Correction for the Front Foot Leg Glance

Error

1. The player plays inside the line of the ball.

2. The batter allows the blade of the bat to get in front of the handle (see figure 7.23).

3. The batter hits across the line of the ball.

4. The batter turns the face of the bat before contact.

Figure 7.23 Allowing the blade to get in front of the handle is a common error.

Correction

1. Practise stepping to cover off stump to a thrown or rolled ball. Keep the head over the bat.

2. Push top hand toward the ball, using a soft grip with the bottom hand.

3. Check backlift as hitting across the line is usually caused by a poor backlift.

4. Strike the ball keeping the front elbow up, or concentrate on striking the ball in the number 9 position.

The Sweep Shot

This stroke is generally reserved for playing spin bowling, played to a ball of good length that is pitched on line from the middle and off stumps to the outside leg stump.

Here are some key points to emphasise with the sweep shot:

- The ball should be hit on the half-volley.
- Make sure that the line of the ball is covered with the pads.
- The bat should be horizontal at impact.
- Roll the wrists.
- Weight should be forward.

Name. Sweep Drill

Organisation. Place a batting tee in an appropriate position or use a ball suspended on a string. Toss a ball from about 10 m away to land just outside the leg stump and on a good length. See figure 7.24. Vary the line of the throw.

Figure 7.24 Sweep drill.

Error Detection and Correction for the Sweep Shot

Error

1. The batter fails to bring the weight over the front knee.

2. The batter is not getting the front leg in line with the ball.

3. The batter is playing the ball with an angled bat.

4. Cramped arm positioning is causing a scooplike shot.

Correction

1. Use markers or cut-out footprints to establish the correct position.

2. Position the tee to make the batter stretch forward.

3. Have the batter position his or her body weight over the front knee and play the shot with a restricted backswing.

4. Show players video footage of their batting, indicate errors, and physically—by holding their arms or the bat—show them the correct swing.

Front Foot Drives

The square drive, off drive, on drive, and cover drive are all played with a vertical swing of the bat to a ball well pitched up. Junior coaches should encourage their players to step to a spot just inside the line of the ball with the head and eyes as close to over the line of the ball as possible. Remember, you are aiming to get your players to step just inside the line, not toe the line. In other words, phrases such as 'step to the ball' can be slightly misleading. At the point of contact there should be minimal distance between bat and pad.

Emphasise these key points when teaching front foot drives:

- Play to a full pitch ball.
- Move in a manner similar to that of a front foot defence, with a full swing of the bat.
- Accelerate during the downswing.
- Keep hands forward, with the top hand in control.

- Make contact with the ball with the full face of the bat, with the front elbow well up.
- Follow through.

Front Foot Driving Drills

When practising front foot driving drills, use the following sequence:

- Stationary ball
- Dropped ball
- Lobbed ball

Name. Tee and Marker (low tee driving)

Organisation. The batter steps forward and hits through the ball. The fielder returns the ball. See figure 7.25.

Variations

- Vary the marker position (off, on, straight drive).
- The batter hits on drive, then off drive (in order).
- The batter hits on drive, off drive, then straight drive (in order).
- The batter's partner drops the ball from shoulder height.

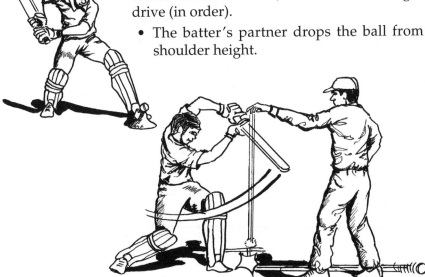

Figure 7.25 Tee and marker drill: the batter *(a)* steps forward and *(b)* hits through the ball.

- The partner lobs the ball from 5 m (check safety—young players should be using soft balls, or at least wearing helmets).
- The partner bounces the ball from 10 m (check safety).
- The ball is dribbled along the ground, then hit (no tee).
- To practise driving a spinner, take three steps out to the tee to drive.
- Rotate the direction of the drive after every hit.

Error Detection and Correction for Front Foot Drives

Error

1. The batter displays incorrect backlift, such as pickup to point rather than first slip.

2. Pickup occurs too late.

3. The initial step with the front foot is too short.

4. The batter is stepping too late, that is, the desired sequence of lift, step, and swing is incorrect.

5. The batter's bottom hand is dominant.

6. The batter drops the elbow of the leading arm.

7. The batter leans back on contact with the ball.

8. The batter plays the ball in front of the pads.

Correction

1. The coach stands behind the batter with a hand in place to provide feedback.

2. The coach stands behind the batter and calls 'lift' at the appropriate time.

3. The coach rolls the ball to the batter until an adequate step is displayed.

4. Practise lift, step, and swing in correct sequence but initially with an obvious time gap between each, gradually decreasing that time gap by the speed in which the coach calls, 'Lift, step, swing'.

5. Practise the swing with only the top hand on the bat, then practise the swing with only the top hand and the thumb and index finger on the bat.

Moving Out to Drive

This is an advanced shot, with correct footwork the key to success. The initial step is with the front foot, then the back foot steps behind the front. The front foot then moves again, stepping and extending toward the pitch of the ball. (See figure 7.15 on page 119.)

Error Detection and Correction for Moving Out to Drive

Error

1. The initial step is too short.

2. The batter steps straight down the pitch instead of to the line of the ball.

3. The batter leans back on contact with the ball.

4. The batter plays the ball away from the pad and the body.

Correction

1. The coach makes the player aware of the error and encourages multiple practices of the footwork in the desired manner.

2. For error 2 also, the coach makes the player aware of the error and encourages multiple practices of the footwork in the desired manner.

3. The coach emphasises weight on the front foot when making contact.

4. The player is given a line on the ground on which to step when advancing toward the tee.

Back Foot Shots

These are strokes generally played to balls that are short pitched— that is, the ball is usually bouncing quite high by the time it reaches the batter. There are two main categories of back foot shots: back foot drives, or vertical shots; and horizontal shots, such as cut, pull, and hook shots.

Emphasise the following key points with back foot shots:

- Move the back foot back and across toward the off stump (see figure 7.26).
- The front foot follows back (with downswing) and in line with the body.
- Keep the front elbow high.
- Keep the top hand firm and the bottom hand relaxed.

Figure 7.26 The correct position for back foot shots.

Back Foot Defence

This is the technique preferred when trying to defend short-pitched deliveries that the batter decides need to be hit with caution. See figure 7.27.

Figure 7.27   In the back foot defence, the arms form a number 9.

Back Foot Defence Drills

Name.   Bouncer/Half-Volley

Organisation.   The batter takes up his or her stance. The coach throws a tennis or indoor cricket ball at either bouncer or half-volley length. Continue until the batter can judge the length confidently and make adjustments.

Name.   Right Back

Organisation.   Draw a line 30 cm behind the batting crease. The batter rehearses moving back, placing the foot in line, and keeping side-on. Progress to hitting the ball off a high tee through target markers. Progress to the coach throwing the ball.

Back Foot Leg Glance

The back foot leg glance is a shot played off the back post to a delivery that is usually on or around leg stumps. The ball is deflected off the hip area down toward fine leg.

The following key points are important for the back foot leg glance:

- Assume the same position as for the back defence.
- Hit the ball with the full face of the bat.

- Turn wrists just after contact to allow the ball to deviate toward fine leg.

Back Foot Leg Glance Drills

- Throw balls aimed at or slightly outside leg stump, to pitch just short of a length to bounce between knee and waist height (see figure 7.28).
- Net practice—in the nets balls are thrown or delivered by bowlers (or a bowling machine) in the appropriate position for the batter to employ the leg glance.

Figure 7.28 Back foot leg glance drill.

Error Detection and Correction for Back Foot Leg Glance

Error

1. The batter plays the ball outside the line of the body.

2. The batter allows the blade of the bat to precede the handle.

3. The batter faces square on to the line of the ball.

4. The batter plays across the line of the ball.

Correction

1. Practise the 9 drill (see figure 7.27). Place the front leg in line with the delivery (use soft ball).

2. Relax the grip of the bottom hand.

3. Emphasise a practice stepping back with the back foot with the toes of that foot pointing to point.

4. Use a batting tee to improve the batter's timing in turning of the wrists.

Back Foot Drives

Back foot drives are generally played to a ball short in length but one that doesn't bounce very high—usually around shin height. The direction of the hit is aimed at in front of square.

Emphasise these key points for back foot drives:

- The back foot moves back and remains stable.
- Keep arms in close to the body.
- The head remains steady, with eyes level.
- Keep the front elbow high at the point of impact.
- Take a full swing with the bat.

Back Foot Driving Drill

Name. Beat the Fielder

Organisation. Position the fielder in the target area. Bounce the ball to the batter who hits for gap. See figure 7.29.

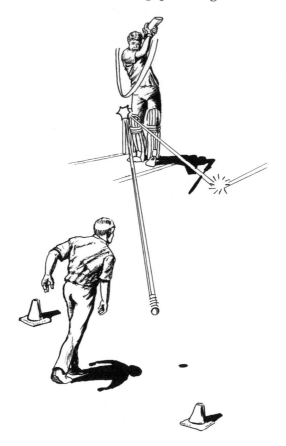

Figure 7.29 Beat the fielder drill.

Error Detection and Correction for Back Foot Drives

Error

1. The batter moves across the crease rather than back to create a front-on position.

2. The batter fails to keep the front elbow high.

3. The batter allows the back elbow to move away from the body.

4. The batter backs away and uses a cross-bat position.

5. The batter allows the bottom hand to control the stroke.

6. The batter takes the head back and away from the line of delivery (usually because of fear of the ball).

7. The batter fails to provide a stable base.

Correction

1. Place a marker or footprint in the appropriate position.

2. Practise lifting the bat with the front hand.

3. Practise the stroke close to the net or wall.

4. Use a soft ball until the player gains confidence.

5. Practise lifting the bat with the front hand.

6. Use a soft ball until the player gains confidence.

Pull Shots

This shot is played to a short-pitched ball that bounces to between waist and chest height. The batter should aim to hit the pull shot in front of square leg. Use the following key points:

- The back foot moves back and across to the off side.
- The head must stay steady.
- Fully extend the arms at the ball.
- Rotate the shoulders.
- Take a full swing with the bat.

Pull Shot Drills

Name. High Tee Pulls

Organisation. The batter takes up his or her stance, with markers at square leg (see figure 7.30). The batter hits the ball between two markers (see figure 7.31). The fielder returns the ball. Replace the batter after three attempts. Score one point for each hit between the markers.

Variations

- Shots in front of square, then behind square.
- The ball is lobbed from 5 m.
- The ball is bounced from 10 m.
- Alternate back foot off drives and on drives from underarm deliveries.
- Players rotate positions after their designated amount of hits.

Figure 7.30 High tee pulls drill: batter stance.

Figure 7.31 The batter hits the ball between markers.

Extension Activity. Underarm the ball on full to strike zone for pull, hook, and cut shots from a distance of 8 m. (Lob from a kneeling position.)

Error Detection and Correction for the Pull Shot

Error

1. The batter moves back rather than across to the line of the delivery.
2. The batter moves too far across to the ball on leg stump.
3. The batter fails to shift weight to the front foot.

Correction

1. Use markers or footprints to improve initial movements.
2. Use a place foot/step drill to transfer weight.

The Hook Shot

The footwork for the hook shot is similar to that for the pull shot, but this stroke is usually played to a quicker ball—one that bounces chest height or higher and as a result is usually hit behind square leg.

These key points are important when teaching the hook shot:

- The batter must be able to judge the different length and pace of the ball.
- The hook shot employs the same foot position as the pull shot.
- Get the body inside the line of the ball.
- Hit down on the ball when possible.
- Take a full swing with the bat.
- Finish facing the direction of the hit.

Name. Hook Shot Drill

Organisation. Use the same drill as for the pull shot, but employ a shorter-pitched delivery.

Cut Shot

The cut shot is played to a short-pitched delivery outside the off side. Emphasise these key points:

- Move the back foot across to the off stump, getting the head in line with the ball.
- Turn the front shoulder toward point.
- Swing the bat horizontally, extending the arms at the ball.
- Keep the hands high and do not lean back.

Name.   Cut Shot Drill

Organisation.   Bounce throw, or underarm to zone. Follow the same drill organisation as with the pull shot. See figure 7.32.

Figure 7.32 Cut shot drill.

Running Between Wickets

The art of running between wickets is an area of the game that is often neglected by junior coaches. With improved technique in turning, backing up, and correct calling, young players can add another dimension to their game and have greater enjoyment.

Practise these key points for calling:

- The coach should emphasise to junior players that only three calls are to be made when batting: 'yes', 'no', or 'wait'.

Error Detection and Correction for the Cut Shot

Error

1. The batter slices the ball in the air.

2. The batter hits with the bat at an angle, that is, between horizontal and vertical, often resulting in the ball played onto the stumps.

3. The batter moves the body weight away from the shot rather than into it.

4. The batter steps with the back foot pointing toward cover rather than point, thus restricting the swing and causing the batter to hit toward cover.

Correction

1. Place a ball 30 cm in front of the bowling crease and 30 cm outside the off stump. Player moves back and across, bends knees, and places the bat on the ball.

2. Use repeated underarm deliveries, encouraging the batter to make a higher backlift.

3. Encourage extending the arms to the ball and a full swing of the bat.

4. Place a piece of carpet on the pitch, onto which you want the player to step. After each practice shot, check the player's foot position.

- The striker calls on most occasions.
- The nonstriker calls when the striker is unsighted.

Here are some key points for backing up:

- The nonstriker should be moving forward as the bowler releases the ball.
- As the ball is hit, the nonstriker continues to move forward without propping.

Emphasise these key points for turning:

- Carry the bat in the appropriate hand and slide the bat over the crease.
- The body should be in a low position at the crease to aid in quick turning speed (see figure 7.33).
- Accelerate from the crease like a sprinter.

Figure 7.33 A low position will increase turning speed.

Bowling

All young players should be coached in basic bowling. They should also have the opportunity to try all aspects of bowling—seam, swing, and spin. Coaches are well advised to understand what causes injuries and know how to remediate their players. A level 1 coach's course adequately addresses these situations and provides such information.

Encourage young bowlers to work on a good line and length. However, be aware that insisting that young, fast bowlers forsake speed for line and length may retard the player's progress. Similarly, young spin bowlers should be encouraged to spin the ball hard and then work on line and length.

Key points for learning to bowl include the following:

- Concentrate—focus on the line to bowl.
- Maintain proper balance alignment—that is, keep the arms in close to the body during the run-up, be in posture (the hips and shoulders in the same plane at back foot landing), and the head high and steady with eyes level throughout.
- Generate power through correct technique in the following: (1) Accelerate gradually in the run-up; (2) jump into the delivery stride; (3) pull the front arm strongly down the target line and keep the elbow close to the body; and (4) rotate the arms and shoulders as vertically as possible toward the target.

Basic Bowling

First the coach needs to identify the correct bowling arm. After demonstrating the basic grip (the first two fingers slightly apart on the seam with the thumb on the seam *under* the ball), shown in figure 7.34, use the drills on the next pages to build a bowling action and run-up.

Emphasise these key points for bowling:

- Keep the head steady and the eyes level.
- Transfer weight from the back foot to the front foot.

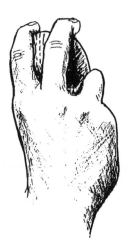

Figure 7.34   Basic bowling grip.

- Pull the front arm down strongly toward the hip.
- The bowling arm should brush the ear and then follow through across the body.

Bowling Drill

Name. Rock and Bowl

Organisation. Stand side-on with feet shoulder-width apart. Hold the front arm high and the bowling hand beside the back leg. Keep feet, hips, and shoulders in line and pointing at the batter. Hold the head level and turned to look at the batter behind the front arm. The bowler rocks his or her weight onto the front foot, then onto the back foot (twice). The arms rotate 180 degrees in time with the transfer of weight. The ball is bowled on the third rock forward; the front arm pulls down past the left hip, with the bowling arm following across the body. See figure 7.35.

Figure 7.35 Rock and bowl drill.

Building an Action

After mastering the technique of releasing the ball with a straight arm, the young bowler should learn the correct lever sequence in progression to develop an efficient action. This is accomplished by starting with the Wrist Flick drill, then adding Gather and Explode, and then adding the rest of the drills up to and excluding Run Up and Bowl. This is an example of reverse teaching and lends itself well to building an action. Reverse teaching is when you analyse all the component parts of a skill (for example, shotput, bowling, throwing, etc.). You then place those component parts in order of first to last (the approach to 'put the shot' to the last component—the release from the hand, for example). You then begin teaching the skill by teaching the last component first and work backwards.

Building an Action Drills

Name. Wrist Flick

Organisation. Stand with legs apart, weight on the front foot, and toe of the back foot on the ground. Tuck the front elbow in beside the front hip. Start with the bowling arm vertical and release the ball with a flick of the wrist. Gradually lower the bowling arm, step by step, keeping the arm straight throughout the swing and release (see figure 7.36).

Figure 7.36 Wrist flick drill.

Name. Gather and Explode

Organisation. Stand with feet together and hands in against the chest. Lift the front knee up close to the body. While stepping forward, unfold the arms by rotating them away from each other (see figure 7.37). When the front arm is up high, deliver the ball using the lever sequence discussed previously. It is important for young bowlers to experience the feel of this activity in that it challenges their natural balance and coordination.

Figure 7.37 Gather and explode drill.

Name.   **Pulling the Chain**

Organisation.   Stand with legs apart, weight on the front foot, and toe of the back foot on the ground. Reach for the sky with the front arm, side-on, and look at the target behind the front elbow, holding the ball next to the back knee (see figure 7.38). 'Pull the chain' by pulling the front elbow into the hip and catapulting the ball around through release. Return to standing position with weight on back foot, then transferring to front foot, 'pulling the chain', and releasing the ball. Follow through with step and full body rotation.

Figure 7.38   Pulling the chain drill.

Walk Up and Bowl

Use the following drill for the walk up and bowl technique. This teaches correct arm position for bowling.

Name.   **Walk Up and Bowl**

Organisation.   Standing approximately three paces from stumps, facing toward batter, walk forward by stepping first with the left leg, then with the right, and again with the left. The next step (right) sees the leg swing across the body to land on and parallel to the bowling crease thus beginning to bring the body into a side-on position. When moving into the side-on position, throw the front arm high and bring the bowling hand to the face (see figure 7.39). On the fifth step (left) commence the arm rotation. Step across the body to face the opposite direction after delivery.

Figure 7.39 Walk up and bowl drill.

Run Up and Bowl

Run up and bowl is another action to practise when teaching bowling. Use the following drill for this technique.

Name.   Run Up and Bowl

Organisation.   Gradually build pace and distance into run-up and delivery. Measure the run by starting from the crease with eyes closed. Run away from the pitch and when it feels right, jump and bowl. Note where the back foot lands, mark the spot, and pace out from there to the crease. Stay in the corridor and move through a straight line. See figure 7.40.

Figure 7.40   Run up and bowl drill.

Pace Bowling

Pace bowling is one of the most important and exciting aspects of cricket. More than any other specific skill in the game, fast bowling requires good technique and a high level of fitness. Injuries in pace bowlers occur as a result of one or a combination of three factors:

1. Poor physical preparation
2. Overbowling at training and matches
3. Poor technique

It is vital that young pace bowlers develop a good technique at an early age. All coaches, especially those dealing with cricketers during the adolescent growth spurt (13–16 years of age), need to understand the fundamentals of good pace bowling technique:

- Momentum—to develop and maintain movement *in the direction of the batter*
- Alignment—to ensure that hips and shoulders face in the same direction at back foot landing (see figures 7.41 and 7.42)
- Stability—to maintain balance and support throughout the delivery stride
- Force absorption—to reduce and release the stresses produced during run-up and delivery

Figure 7.41 Recommended pace bowling technique: alignment at back foot landing *(a)* side-on, *(b)* semi-open, and *(c)* front-on, *(d)* release, and *(e)* follow-through.

Figure 7.42 Common problems with pace bowling technique. 1.) mixed alignment at back foot landing *(a)* shoulders front-on, hips side-on; *(b)* shoulders side-on, hips past side-on; or *(c)* shoulders side-on, hips front-on. 2.) Shoulder counterrotation: the shoulders quickly move from a more front-on position at *(d)* back foot landing, to *(e)* a more side-on position just before front foot landing. Shoulder counterrotation is strongly linked to lower back injuries. 3.) Hyperextension: the back is excessively arched at *(f)* back foot landing and/or during the delivery stride. 4.) Excessive lateral flexion: the trunk is excessively bent sideways at *(g)* ball release.

Wicket Keeping

The wicket keeper provides the focal point of the fielding team. Keeping wickets is a complex, subtle art, but for the purposes of clear coaching we have established some key points in this book that form the basis for wicket keepers at all levels of experience. Key points to consider in wicket keeping include crouch, positioning, glovework, footwork, and concentration.

- *Crouch.* In the crouch position, the keeper should position his or her feet approximately shoulder-width apart. Weight is balanced on the balls of the feet. Gloves are touching the ground with the little fingers together and the palms totally open to the ball, facing the bowler. This position is shown in figure 7.43.

Figure 7.43   The crouch position.

- *Positioning.* Ensure that the keeper has a clear view at delivery and is positioned to take the ball at hip height when standing back to the fast bowlers. When keeping to the spinners, the keeper's feet should be about 50–60 cm back from the stumps with the head outside the line of the stump.

- *Glovework.* With cupped gloves, the keeper should rise with the ball—that is, wait until it bounces. Point the fingers at the ground, at the sky, or sideways (see figure 7.44).

- *Footwork.* When standing back to the faster bowlers, the keeper moves the feet so as to take the ball in line with the inside hip. Keep knees bent throughout the sideways movement. To spinners keep the eyes over the gloves in line with the ball. Move across the crease in a straight line.

- *Concentration.* The great part about wicket keeping is that the keeper is totally involved in the game whilst in the field. This requires enormous concentration, however, and therefore can be extremely taxing, both physically and mentally. It is therefore important that the keeper be able to switch 'on' and 'off'—in other words, be able to focus when the ball is live and relax when it is dead. Switch off completely as the bowler walks back to his or her mark, and switch on sometime after the run-up has commenced but before the ball has been released. Recover from an error through positive thinking and involvement. The coach can assist the young wicket keeper by reminding him or her to recall all the good catches or stumpings

Figure 7.44 When catching, the wicket keeper positions the gloves *(a)* toward the ground, *(b)* toward the sky, or *(c)* sideways.

that he or she has made before, and to rehearse mentally the proper technique to use next time. The wicket keeper is the engine room on the field—the motivator who sets the example with energetic enthusiasm, both during games and at training.

Wicket-Keeping Drills

Drills should simulate match conditions as closely as possible. For example, in Wall Catching (page 158), the wicket keeper should relate the activity to taking the ball in line with the inside hip on the off side or on side, depending on the sideways movement. The coaching points and focus for each activity should be specific to the developmental needs of the keepers (e.g., their obvious weaknesses) and selected from the key points of the relevant sections of this book. In all the drills, the major focus is the ball. Have your keeper watch it right into the gloves in all activities.

Name.   Half-Volleys

Purpose.   This drill establishes effective footwork and glovework as well as the focus required in a game, such as a right-handed batter missing the ball outside off stump or leg stump.

Organisation.   The wicket keeper is back in a semi-crouch position. Throw to hitter on the bounce, move to take catch. See figure 7.45.

Figure 7.45   Half-volleys drill.

Variations

- Work leg side/off side (10 each).
- Vary the distance back the keeper stands.

Name.   Fast Bowling

Organisation.   The keeper takes the ball in line with the inside hip, with weight on the balls of the feet, gloves low, and movement strong and well balanced. Employ the crossover or sidestepping method of foot movement. See figure 7.46.

Figure 7.46   Fast bowling drill.

Name.   **High Balls**

Purpose. This drill helps maintain the keeper's confidence in taking running high balls, especially in windy conditions. The keeper is back in the crouch position. The ball is lobbed in high over the wicket keeper's head (see figure 7.47). The keeper turns, calls, sprints, and catches the ball.

Figure 7.47   High balls drill.

Variations

- The keeper begins facedown, on his or her back, or kneeling.
- The ball is hit rather than thrown.

Name.   **Stumping**

Purpose. The purpose of this drill is to ensure that the keeper only watches the ball and doesn't react suddenly when it hits an obstruction or just misses it. The coach places the bat face down on a good length. The thrower bounces the ball to the keeper, who is crouched behind the stumps. See figure 7.48. The keeper completes stumping.

Figure 7.48   Stumping drill.

Variations

- Change the pace, length, and spin of the throws.
- Place the stump as an obstruction at various lengths and lines.

- Have the batter stand in position and play inside and outside the line.
- Use cricket, golf, and tennis balls.
- Use shadow batting routines: a batter simulates attempts at striking the ball, although intentionally missing.

Name. Nicks

Purpose. In this drill, the keeper focuses only on the ball, not on the swinging bat; he or she must stay low, focus, and move powerfully sideways. The drill simulates the 'nick' in the game and allows the keeper to practise glovework.

Organisation. The wicket keeper and slip crouch in position. The batter nicks the ball from the thrower, and the fielders catch (see figure 7.49).

Variations

- Change the pace of the throws and the depth of the catches; employ both underarm and overarm throws.
- Have two competing teams on opposite sides of the hitter—'nicks' and 'glides'.

Figure 7.49 Nicks drill.

Name. Slips Cradle

Purpose. The goal of this drill is to produce a general rhythm of slip work and to develop slip patterns and understanding for the cordon who will be together in the match.

Organisation. The ball is thrown into the cradle. The keeper moves from a crouch position to take the catch (see figure 7.50).

Variations

- Use the roller instead of the cradle.
- Have one slip next to the keeper to develop understanding between them.
- Vary the pace and angle of the throws.

Figure 7.50 Slips cradle drill.

Name. Wall Catching

Purpose. This drill helps keepers to develop effective sideways movement for quick and slow bowlers, to learn to cushion the ball sufficiently with the hands and watch the ball as it enters the hands, and to employ mental imagery for the many tight situations that will be encountered in upcoming matches.

Organisation. The keeper stands square to a wall in semicrouch position with inners on and throws a golf ball to rebound first off the wall, then off the concrete (or vice versa) before catching it (see figure 7.51). He or she continues, moving sideways along the wall and back.

Variations

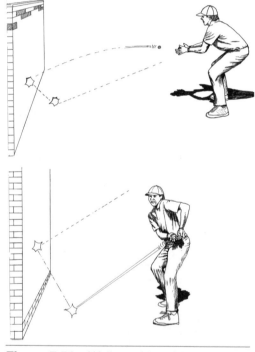

- Change the angle, height, and pace of the throws.
- Change the distance from the wall so the keeper can take diving and reflex catches.
- Place sand, stones, stump, or a bat in the bounce zone.
- Utilise a thrower from behind the keeper.
- Use a tennis ball.

Figure 7.51 Wall catching drill.

Fielding

Although coaches often neglect to give serious attention to fielding drills, fielding is as important as batting and bowling. There now exist many varied and interesting drills that simulate the numerous situations that arise during a game of cricket. You need to provide quality and quantity in your practice drills. Players should be involved in quality activities and get plenty of turns at that activity. The old drill where one player hits the ball to a group of players standing in a semicircle will not adequately prepare your players for match play.

The following are key points to ground fielding:

- Maintain a low body position, bending the knees.
- Watch the ball into the hands.
- Return to the keeper on the full.
- Communicate with teammates.

Fielding the Ball

The coach should instill into the players the importance of fielding as they spend about 80 percent of their time doing exactly that. Every player should aim at becoming as competent at fielding as he or she is at batting and bowling.

The key points in fielding the ball are as follows:

- Attack the ball.
- Reach out and 'suck' the ball in with soft hands.
- Return the ball with a flat throw or a clear bounce to the keeper (or the fielder at the bowler's end).

Fielders away from the bat (i.e., those not in the slips or in close-to-the-bat positions) move in with the bowler. At the moment the ball is about to be hit, the fielders should take short, quick steps, preparing to move left, right, forward, or back. The fielder should keep body weight low to the ground and on the inside of the balls of the feet. Adjust the body position for a clean pickup, watch the ball into the hand, and keep the eyes and the head steady. The fielder can maximise anticipation by watching the batter's stance, footwork, backlift, and bat angles.

In attacking fielding, the fielder approaches the ball and adjusts the feet to be on either side of the ball when it arrives. The fielder's head should be in line with the ball, with hands extended out to meet the ball (see figure 7.52). Keeping the elbows bent and with 'soft hands', suck the ball into the stomach region, then take the ball away in the throwing hand ready to throw.

In defensive fielding, the body should be used as the second defence. Avoid being late in positioning the body and bending the knees and hips as low as is practicable. The fielder must keep his or her eyes on the ball, allowing the hands to 'give' with the ball.

Figure 7.52 Correct position for attacking fielding.

Throwing the Ball

Although throwing is an important skill in cricket, modern cricket coaches rarely teach correct throwing technique. Throwing is therefore quite often one of the weakest skills in players from junior to senior levels. Even athletes with strong arms very often have poor throwing technique. So set aside a time during each practice session to work on throwing. Bad habits are difficult to break, so make sure players are performing the skill the way you are coaching it, and try not to allow them to develop bad habits in the first place.

Good throwing technique helps to increase players' speed, accuracy, and distance and helps to prevent injury, especially to the elbow and shoulder joint.

Underarm Throwing

Underarm throws are used in close-to-the-wicket run-out situations. The return may be to the wicket keeper or the fielder or bowler at the bowler's end, depending on at which end the run out is to be effected. The thrower's feet point in the direction of the throw; the hips and shoulders face the target.

The thrower steps with the foot on the side of the throwing arm level with the ball, steps onto the foot on the nonthrowing side, and releases. Stay low on release and extend the arm and hand at the target (see figure 7.53).

Overarm or Long-Arm Throwing

Many forms and variations of throwing are executed in different circumstances. We suggest, however, that the young cricketer learn

Figure 7.53 Underarm throwing.

Error Detection and Correction for Underarm Throwing

Error

1. The thrower bends the elbow of the throwing arm on release.

2. The thrower stands up on release.

Correction

1. Extend the fingers towards the stumps on release.

2. Keep low or crouched on and after release (i.e., don't stand up too soon).

the overarm throw first, because doing so will result in a greater transfer of skills to the short-arm or snap throw as well as to other infield throws that rely on accuracy and speed of release.

• *The grip.* The player holds the ball across the seam with the middle and index finger on top and the thumb underneath. The two fingers on top should be one finger-width apart (see figure 7.54). The player holds the ball on the finger pads, making sure not to hold it too tightly. When released, the ball should come off the pads of the middle and index finger last.

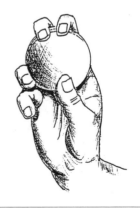

Figure 7.54 Correct grip for underarm throwing.

- *Preparation.* Bringing the throwing arm back and up, the player turns so the front shoulder is pointed at the target. At this point the player's weight is on the back foot. The opposite (nonthrowing hand) is pointed at the target. The arm extends behind the body with the wrist cocked and the elbow bent.

- *Release.* The player now steps toward the target with the lead foot (i.e., the foot on the opposite side to the throwing arm; the left foot for right-arm throws). As the front (lead) foot touches the ground, the hips are turned so that the throwing side hip rotates and drives toward the target. The player transfers his or her weight onto the front foot, pulling down with the front elbow into the hip. The throwing arm comes through with the elbow leading the action (the elbow should be no lower than the ear), that is, the player moves the throwing elbow to the target before the hand. The throwing hand should follow through to the opposite side of the body.

- *Follow-through.* When the ball is released, the player's weight is well balanced on the front foot (or the left foot for right-arm throwers), with that leg slightly bent. Follow through by stepping through to finish with the throwing side shoulder, hip, and foot pointing at the target. The throwing arm finishes past the hip on the other side of the body.

Overarm Throwing Drills

Name. Wrist and Finger Flick

Organisation. Partners sit 3 m apart. Each partner holds his or her own wrist with the nonthrowing hand. The partners bounce the ball to each other with a flicking action (see figure 7.55).

Figure 7.55 Wrist and finger flick drill.

Name. **Elbow Flick**

Organisation. Partners sit 5 m apart. Each partner holds his or her throwing arm triceps with the nonthrowing hand. The partners bounce the ball to each other using the elbow, wrist, and fingers (see figure 7.56).

Figure 7.56 Elbow flick drill.

Name. **Shoulder Rotation**

Organisation. Partners kneel on back knee 10 m apart, throwing the ball to each other. Finish with throwing shoulder pointing to target (see figure 7.57). Focus on technique rather than power.

Figure 7.57 Shoulder rotation drill.

Name. Hip Rotation

Organisation. Partners stand 15 m apart, each with front shoulder, hip, and foot pointing to the target. Partners bounce the ball to each other, stepping through to finish with the throwing shoulder, hip, and foot pointing at the target (see figure 7.58). Once the players master hip rotation, have them concentrate on digging the front arm in beside the front hip to generate power.

Figure 7.58 Hip rotation drill.

Name. Crow Hop

Organisation. The player watches the ball closely into the hands while keeping the body low to the ground. Draw the ball into the stomach area. Skip forward by bringing the foot on the throwing side past and in front of the other foot (see figure 7.59). Step with the nonthrowing-side leg whilst pushing off with the opposite foot (the right leg for right-handers). Throw the ball over the top.

Figure 7.59 Crow hop drill.

Using the Cutoff Player

The cutoff player is one who positions himself or herself between the player fielding the ball (usually near the boundary) and the pitch. With long returns from the outfield a player should not overextend and may use either a relay to throw to a player midway to the wicket (particularly if the ball is new) or a bounce throw, where the ball is skimmed low so that it lands 3–5 m before the stumps and the bounce can be easily gathered to allow for an easy run out. See figure 7.60.

Figure 7.60 Using a cutoff player.

Name. Relay Throw Practice

Organisation. Players concentrate on throwing accurately to the relay thrower's throwing shoulder, keeping in mind whether that player throws with the right or the left arm.

Catching

Two acceptable techniques are used for taking high outfield catches. The first is where the fielder cups his or her hands under the ball with elbows tucked into the sides. Hands should be positioned around eye level and no lower than chin level (see figure 7.61).

Figure 7.61 Catching the ball with elbows tucked into the sides.

In the second technique, the fielder pushes his or her elbows away from the body, inverting the palms upward. The palms should be positioned above eye level, allowing the player to watch the ball into the hands (see figure 7.62).

Figure 7.62 Catching the ball pushing the elbows away from the body.

Both methods are effective and, like all skills of cricket, must be practised often. Either method can be applied to the ball that is hit high into the air.

Key points for catching include the following:

- Move quickly to the line of the ball, putting the hands in a high, comfortable position.
- Watch the ball into the hands.
- Use the elbows as shock absorbers.

Slips Catching

When in slips fielders need to have quick, soft hands, enabling them to catch instinctively. Concentrate on these key points:

- Practise safety rolls, which is basically a side-roll in a tucked position.
- Block impact of landing on the ground, usually by taking part of the weight with the free hand.
- Shoulder and arm rolls to cushion impact. These are employed to avoid landing on the point of the shoulder or elbow. The catcher takes his or her initial weight on the forearm before completing a safety roll. With shoulder rolls, the leading arm and shoulder are tucked under just before landing with the player rolling onto his or her back avoiding arm or shoulder contact with the ground.
- Use gym mats or sand pits in training.

Diving in the Slips Drills

Name. Slips Catching

Organisation. The ball can be lobbed only from below knee height. Each pair must try not to allow the ball to land in their section. See figure 7.63.

Name. Diving Pairs

Organisation. Position mats on both sides of catchers. Catch thrown over mat (particular side initially); extend distance so that the catcher has farther to dive, and then throw either side (see figure 7.64). When advanced, score points for dropped catch or ball landing on opponent's mat.

Figure 7.63 Slips catching drill.

Figure 7.64 Diving pairs drill.

Name. Pair Lines

Organisation. Partners stand opposite each other, with one ball for each pair. The pair take as many catches as possible in a given time (e.g., 1 minute).

Fielding Strategies Drills

Tactical simulations to improve fielding could include the following:

- Positions in the field, angles to batsmen, and so on
- Walking in with the bowler
- Diving in the field
- Saving singles or giving singles

- Backing up
- Throwing at the stumps
- Close-to-the-wicket catching
- Bat-pad fielding
- Outfield catches
- Coping with the sun
- Long throws
- Relay throws
- Sliding stops
- Run outs (with batsmen)

Name. Multiple-Ball Throws

Organisation. Place balls inside markers in a diamond pattern. Place the target stump in front of the wicket keeper. The fielder runs out from the stump and throws the ball, in order, at the stump (see figure 7.65). Score one point for each hit.

Variations

- Vary the number of balls.
- Vary the order of retrieval.

Figure 7.65 Multiple-ball throws drill.

- Vary the starting point and distances.
- Use both overarm and underarm throws.
- Vary the marker positions.
- Vary the number of stumps to be hit.

Name.   **Run-a-Two Run Outs**

Organisation.   Have one team of runners and one team of fielders. On calling 'yes', the first runner sets off for a two; the first fielder runs to the ball and throws to the receiver (see figure 7.66). Each player then moves to the opposite group to attempt the other skill. Score one point for a run out or a safe run.

Figure 7.66   Run-a-two run outs drill.

Name. **Sprint Off**

Organisation. Have two competing lines of numbered fielders. The coach calls out a number (see figure 7.67). The first fielder of that number to return the ball to the wicket keeper scores a point for that team.

Variation. Fielders begin by standing, then sitting, then lying down.

Figure 7.67 Sprint off drill.

Name. **Hand Grenades**

Organisation. Fielders try to land the ball on full in another team's zone. Score one point for each landing. See figure 7.68.

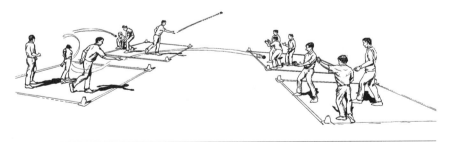

Figure 7.68 Hand grenades drill.

Variations

- Use multiple balls.
- Vary the number of players on each team.
- Vary the size of the zones.
- Vary the distance between zones.

Name. Triangle Target Hitting

Organisation. Place stumps in a triangle with run-in (the starting position for fielders) markers positioned for the fielders. The wicket keeper rolls the ball out to the first fielder (position marker 1), who aims at stumps, backed up by the next fielder (position marker 2), who aims at the next stump (see figure 7.69). The backup returns the ball to the wicket keeper. Each fielder rotates to the next marker position after throwing. A hit scores one point.

Variations

- The ball is hit, rather than rolled, to the first fielder.
- Vary the distance between stumps for overarm and underarm throws.

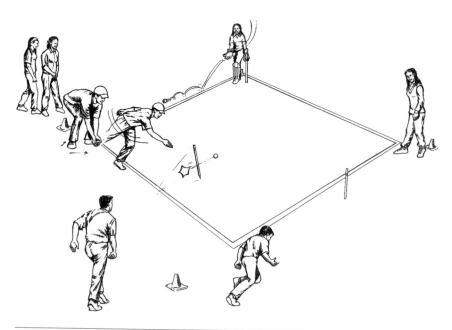

Figure 7.69 Triangle target hitting drill.

Name. Field Ball

Organisation. Have two sets of goals 30–40 m apart. The goal defenders' semicircle is a 3–5 m radius. The aim is to score a goal by rolling the ball from outside the goal zone through the goal. Players may roll the ball to teammates; there is no off side (see figure 7.70). Players cannot run with the ball but can run to receive it. The goal shot must be with the non-dominant hand, underarm; there is one goalkeeper per team.

Variations

- Use catches rather than rolls, using one hand or both hands.
- Use one-bounce throws.
- Vary underarm and overarm throws.

Figure 7.70 Field ball drill.

Name. Caught and Bowled

Organisation. Players employ a normal run-up and delivery without a ball. The coach hits the ball off the tee for players to catch just after the simulated delivery.

Cricket is a game not only of physical skills but of strategies and tactics as well. In this unit, we will look at setting both team and individual goals and discuss the differences between achievement goals and performance goals. We will help you determine to what extent you should emphasise one type of goal over the other and show you the advantages and disadvantages of each.

Preparation and Attitude

Basic psychological principles are important in cricket coaching. A fundamental understanding of these helps you to do the following:

- Highlight your role as a coach in facilitating learning
- Teach the fundamental principles of learning and reinforcement
- Create a learning environment through the reflective use of organisation and communication skills
- Introduce the principles of match preparation and basic tactics (the degree of involvement will depend on the age and experience of your players)

Organisation

Successful clubs and teams have plans that

- are appropriate to the age, skills experience, and aspirations of the players;
- encourage a sense of purpose and confidence amongst all members of the club or team;
- provide enjoyment and an environment where all players (especially at training) experience some sense of achievement each session;
- make training an enjoyable experience; and
- make your expectations, including basic standards and results, clearly understood by all.

Setting Goals

For the coach, the process of setting goals is the first and most important step in planning. Clear goals or objectives are essential for a coach to create a successful programme. These goals will generally cover each of two categories: achievement and performance.

Achievement Goals

Achievement goals provide motivation and can be long term, such as to win the premiership or to play at state or national level, or short term, such as to win the next game.

The goal of winning should never come at the expense of a young player's skill development. As a coach, you should provide goals that are appropriate to the age and experience of your players. For example, the younger the players, the shorter the time frame for goals and the less ambitious the goals should be.

Goals should also be attainable. If the goals are set too high and are not achieved, the young cricketer will probably go through a period of demotivated participation or, at worst, give up the sport.

Performance Goals

It's important to remember that performance goals are more under the control of the young cricketer than are achievement goals and with that in mind, the coach of younger players should place greater focus on these. Performance goals (e.g., bowling a leg spinner) describe the processes or actions that lead to the achievement goals. They differ in that they relate only to performance and are unlikely to change greatly, except perhaps to be upgraded periodically.

Again, failure to reach performance goals will probably result in a period of demotivation for players. *Beware:* Many coaches fail to gain full benefits from goal setting because they do not involve the players in the process. Even at the younger ages, it is valuable for you to create within your players a feeling of ownership for the goals.

Principles of Effective Goal Setting

Numerous research studies have shown that the effective use of goal setting can markedly improve performance. As coach, you can ensure that goal setting is effective by following these guidelines:

- Be specific; the goals should be clear and written down. With the coach guiding the group, allow the players to come up with some specific goals. Make sure they are written down, and then display them in the clubrooms. Players will take goal setting more seriously if they have some ownership of the goals.

- The goals should be measurable—for example, bowlers shall attempt to bowl no more than one ball per over down the leg side at training.

- Make sure the goals are challenging for everyone. The goals set should include some that the lesser-skilled players can achieve and some that are much more challenging for the highly talented team members. This will give the average players a sense of achievement and the best players something to aim for.

- Flexibility in goal setting is vital. You need to alter goals as circumstances change. For example, early in the season the goal for U12 opening bowlers might be that they bowl four out of six balls per over outside the off stump or on the wickets. As the players improve throughout the season, you may wish to change this to five out of six.

- When you have set multiple goals, they should be listed in order of priority. In general, there should be more than one goal for a performance. The ambition in performing should always be to achieve a number of outcomes rather than a single goal outcome. For example, if the goal was to bowl more 'dof' balls (balls that aren't scored off) than the opposition, or to take more singles when batting, the outcomes would be more pressure on the opposition batting, more pressure on the opposition fielders and bowlers, and ultimately winning the game.

Practical Goal Setting

Practical goal setting can affect quality of performance and is therefore important from the perspective of both the team and the individual players. Cricketers without team or individual goals will lack direction, purpose, and an adequate, clear form of assessment.

In the following section we attempt to give coaches some direction in the areas of practical goal setting for both the team and the individual.

The junior cricket coach should direct his or her players to develop goals and a plan for achieving them. This includes a list of standards for such area as

- dress—for example, all players will play with their shirts tucked in;
- practice behaviour—players shall, within reason, be punctual;
- match behaviour—for example, no player, when fielding or bowling, shall make any degrading comments toward the opposition batting team; and
- off-field behaviour—no player shall be involved in conduct that may bring the club or themselves into disrepute.

Team

The junior cricket coach should meet with the team to discuss goals and involve the players in developing an agreed-on plan for making improvements in key areas. Again, it is important to give the players some ownership of the goals set. To prevent any confusion, the coach should write down the team rules, goals, and standards and distribute them to all players in addition to displaying them in a prominent place. Regularly meet with the players to review their progress and provide feedback on performance. Goals will become so much more relevant to young players if the coach praises the team when these goals are achieved. Positive feedback is one of the coach's most powerful tools.

Individual

The coach can help the young cricketer develop a personal goal plan, including both short-term and long-term goals. (This can be closely associated or linked to the next section on routines and preparation.) For example, a short-term personal goal could be for the young player to aim to score 10 runs. Once that 10 runs has been achieved, the player tries again for another 10, and so on. Another short-term goal might be to better his or her best or highest score. A long term goal could be to reach a higher batting average than that of the previous season.

The coach should offer advice on goals, particularly with regard to what is challenging but also what is realistic. Have each player develop a personal improvement plan based on areas that you see needing attention. An example of this might be a young batter who picks her bat up toward point. Obviously, this will limit her ability to drive on the off side, and a much straighter backlift is desirable. Offering advice on a remedial practice drill that the player can work on alone will be of great assistance to the player who really wants to improve.

A corrective drill for the fault just mentioned would be to hang a plastic bottle from a tree or clothesline at just above stump height. Repeating the backlift over and over again to hit the bottle, without looking, will provide feedback and gradually execute the appropriate change.

Review the individual's plan regularly and ask the player for his or her assessment of progress. As a guideline, do this once a month, then suggest changes as required.

Preparation

Top-level cricketers follow certain pregame and within-game routines. You can help your players develop effective routines by explaining their importance and then following the guidelines in this section of the text.

It is of vital importance to be prepared. For example, a player about to open the batting who discovers he has left his favourite bat at home is unlikely to perform at his best because he will lose focus on the task ahead. Make it a point that players should prepare their gear, clothes, bats, shoes, hats, and so forth the night before the game and have it all packed and ready to go the day before the match.

Pregame Routines

The effective coach creates a team system based around routines for the following areas:

- Clear arrangements for arriving at the ground or a common meeting place for transport.
- Team meetings to discuss strategies, such as routinely meeting 30 minutes before the game to inspect the ground, pitch, or weather conditions. Revise any team plan that has been considered and discuss what is required of the bowlers, where to bowl to certain batters, and how to field.
- Follow this meeting with a general warm-up and stretching exercises, then engage the group in some minor fielding and batting drills.
- The final discussion could follow, but remember to leave time for the players to do their own preferred preparation, especially if they are relatively experienced. Younger, inexperienced players should be guided through their preparation to keep them physically and mentally ready when the game begins.

Within-Game Routines

Within-game routines fall into two broad, overlapping categories: team routines and individual routines.

Team Routines

Young players, whether they like it or not, need to have a set of boundaries to operate within. They generally conform to routines that they acknowledge as part of the game, especially if they have seen the test team engage in a similar activity. Therefore, walking out together and throwing the ball from player to player could be the first part of the team routine. Here are some other options:

- At the end of an over the team, as one, runs to change ends, and all encourage the bowler at the top of the bowler's run.
- When a wicket falls, everyone runs in to huddle, congratulating anyone who had a hand in the dismissal and issuing words of encouragement to each other in regard to the anticipation of the next wicket.
- The incoming batter hits the ball through the covers. The ball is retrieved and thrown to the bowler's end, where several fielders

have moved to back up the throw. The rest of the team acknowledges their efforts.

- Before passing the ball on to the bowler, the last player to handle it gives it a healthy polish on the trousers to help maintain the shine.

- At a break or at the end of an innings, the batters walk back together, a physical sign of oneness, of being a team. Likewise, the batting side on the boundary all sit together, applauding any good strokes and offering encouragement.

These are but a few ideas. Most of these routines are minor aspects of cricket, but they can set the standard for the team's total performance and as such are very important.

Individual Routines

Here are some examples of individual routines your players could adopt:

- The batter starting an innings walks to the centre, looks to the sky to become accustomed to the light, and then takes guard and looks around the ground to assess the field placements. The batter then faces up to the bowler with the primary aim of watching the ball leave the bowler's hand.

- Between deliveries, the bowler may reflect on a preconceived plan, mentally rehearse the release of the ball, or consider any observed flaw in the batter's technique. On reaching his or her bowling marker, the bowler gives the ball a bit of polish, positions the fingers to the appropriate grip, and commences the run-up.

- Wicket keepers have their routines and idiosyncrasies as well, such as tapping their fingers into the ends of their gloves, doing some slight stretches, adjusting their pads, calling out a few words of encouragement, and then getting into position as the bowler begins to run in.

These are just a few, but individual routines include all the things that you as a coach want the players to do consistently during the game.

Coaches can help players develop effective routines by highlighting those behaviours that help to produce results. For example, players can use the time between deliveries to plan and to polish the ball, or young players can throw the ball around the field to keep the ball off the ground (especially on early spring mornings, when the ground is often wet after a heavy dew).

Tactics

Tactics can play a major role in cricket at both senior and junior levels for both players and coaches. It is the coach's responsibility to schedule productive time to develop skill, understanding, and effective practical application of both attacking and defensive tactics. Deciding which tactics to adopt can often spell the difference between success and failure.

The Toss

The captain who wins the toss must decide whether to bat or to bowl. The junior coach should guide the young captain by explaining all the factors that should be considered, such as the state of the ground, the state of the wicket (if on turf), the length of the grass, weather conditions, and so forth. We recommend, however, that after giving the young player the important factors to consider, you leave it up to him or her to make the final decision.

A team's player personnel may well have a bearing on the final decision. For instance, on a humid, overcast day a team with a good swing bowler may be advantaged by bowling first because the cricket balls are more conducive to swinging in these conditions.

Batting

Organising the batting order is usually the job of the coach and the captain, although the aim should be to attack as much as possible. The most difficult time to bat is early in the innings when the ball is new and hard and most likely to move around in the air and off the pitch.

The opening batters should therefore usually be the safer batters in the team so as to get the innings off to a good start and wear the shine off the ball, making it safer for the more attacking, aggressive batters farther down the order. Players should be aware of the importance of short singles so they learn to mix their game up. They should aim to set up partnership. For example, aim for each pair to form a partnership of 20 runs.

Depending on the match situation, it may be necessary for a batter to attack the bowling or to defend and not take any risks of losing wickets. The junior cricket coach needs to point out what approach to apply depending on the situation.

Note: Where very young players are involved, such as U12s, it's a good idea to rotate the batting order each game so that players get to bat in different positions and a few gifted players don't dominate the batting.

Bowling

The bowling attack is a cricket phase; stick to it and attack on almost all occasions. Use pace bowlers in short spells, not only for their physical well-being but also because they will be more effective in short bursts where they can bowl 'flat out'.

The fast, medium-pace, and off-spin bowlers should aim to pitch the ball just outside or on the off stump, slightly short of a length. This is the area that is most likely to dismiss a batter. Balls that go down leg side are easily avoided and often go for easy runs.

Defensive bowling requires deeper field placements, with the bowler pitching the ball up, outside off stump. Avoid bowling anything short that can be easily hit to the boundary.

In the Field

Junior coaches need to pay attention to the subtleties of team tactics in the field and gradually develop them with their teams. Players must become confident in attacking the ball and competent at intercepting the ball and returning it to the keeper or bowler. Run outs and match-winning catches do not just happen. Each batter is different and should receive special attention with respect to field placings. The most obvious tactic is field placings: fielders may be positioned to cut off a batter's favourite shot or a gap left in the field to invite a rash shot. A speedy fielder may be placed in a specific position with the aim of making a stop and returning the ball quickly to the stumps, or a left-handed fielder may be positioned at a particular point (to the right-hand batter) because he or she is more capable of throwing to either end. Whatever happens, being in the field can be great fun as well as challenging exercise.

Let Everyone Participate

It has been said that the quality of a team is best measured by its least-skilled player. That may or may not be true, but a group of young players all of whom can contribute in some way will go a long way to creating a successful and happy cricket team.

As we said in Unit 2, participation is at least as important as success to young players. So even if it means losing a game or two, give all your players roughly equivalent opportunities to bat, bowl, wicket keep, and field over a number of sessions.

Apply this principle during training as well. Letting everyone play and not stressing winning at all costs gives your players the opportunity to blossom and test their abilities at cricket.

*You'll find
other outstanding
sport resources at*

www.humankinetics.com

In the U.S. call

1-800-747-4457

Australia 08 8277 1555
Canada 1-800-465-7301
Europe .... +44 (0) 113 278 1708
New Zealand 0064 9 448 1207

HUMAN KINETICS
The Premier Publisher for Sports and Fitness
P.O. Box 5076 • Champaign, IL 61825-5076 USA